YOU DON'T SAY!

YOU DON'T SAY!

OVER 1,000 HILARIOUS SPORTS QUOTES AND QUIPS

Hartley Miller

Edited by Jim Swanson

Andrews McMeel Publishing

Kansas City

 For information, write Andrews McMeel Publishing, an Andrews McMeel Universal company, 4520 Main Street, Kansas City, Missouri 64111.

05 06 07 08 09 MLT 10 9 8 7 6 5 4 3 2 1

ISBN-13: 978-0-7407-5487-6
ISBN-10: 0-7407-5487-4

Library of Congress Control Number: 2005922480

Book design by Lisa Martin
Illustrations by G. J. Lesniewicz

www.andrewsmcmeel.com

For Brenda, Lucas, and Lexine

I know you like to read,
so here's a chuckle from me to you.
Thanks for being such
"GOOD SPORTS."

This is also dedicated to
Harold Miller and Pamela Smith.

CONTENTS

CONTENTS

PREFACE

Not unlike millions of other people across the globe, sports can really get me going. I've been fortunate to make a living because of sports, while at the same time not having to deal with the pressures of competing.

As a sportscaster, delivering scores and stories to listeners on morning and afternoon broadcasts has helped brighten my day in a job I still truly enjoy. Early in my career, I was encouraged to come up with a "kicker"—a calling card that would suitably conclude each sportscast, something that would enlighten and entertain. Hence the beginnings of "Sports Quote of the Day."

For many years, I have been scouring news wires, newspapers, magazines, and the Internet for "zinger" sports quotes. Along the way, I was given more sage advice that the quotes should be put into book form.

A rule I've followed from the beginning has been to be true to the source and spirit of each quote, whether read on the air or repeated in this book. Every effort has been made to properly attribute each quote to the original source, in context, with a suitable explanation of the circumstances surrounding each comment.

Many of the quotes are funny, side-splitters that could very well make you laugh out loud. Some are perplexing, corny, or even controversial. I'm sure you may even moan and groan from time to time. If you find a smile creeping across your face because a sportswriter or comedian said something funny, then this book is a success. After all, it's meant to be a fun read. But it's even better if you come away from reading this book with a greater understanding of sports. I know I have learned a lot through my search for entertaining sports quotes.

The most important point of this book, and indeed my "Sports Quote of the Day" feature on the radio, is for the material to speak to people who are not die-hard sports fans. There is much to learn about life and about people in these pages. Sports, after all, is about personalities, people from all walks of life who simply have the distinction of being involved.

I have been asked which of these quotes is my favorite—personally, I really don't have any one or two favorites. However, I would like to thank the comedians, athletes, coaches, executives, media hounds, and fans who are featured time and again in this book—for their wit and for providing insight through their quick tongues.

This project definitely isn't a one-man show. Jim Swanson (editor), Andrea Walker (creative), and George

Lesniewicz (artist) have all been major contributors. If you don't like what you read, blame them . . . and if you do enjoy, I'll take the credit.

I don't want this to sound like an Oscar acceptance speech, but thanks to a number of other people who offered encouragement in their own way: Greg Tyndall, Roger Knox, Charles Buchon, Jason Peters, Fil (J.D.) Decarvalho, Tom Dawson, Nevio Rossi, Tim Tschampa, and Brian McKinnon, who will be delighted to see his name in print. As much as I tell my coworkers (especially the riffraff and the folks in the newsroom) that they have a way of getting on my nerves at times–I would still like to thank my fellow employees for their support and program directors Gary Russell and Darren Coogan for the extra airtime. The 94X/Wolf staff can act as great guinea pigs when testing out quotes.

Last but not least, a big thanks to Francesca Vrattos of Vrattos Literary Agency, because this project wouldn't be the success it is without your valued guidance. To the professionals at Andrews McMeel, thanks for sharing my vision.

To conclude, I hope you're entertained, as *You Don't Say* is my way of wishing you a great day.

CHAPTER 1

BEST OF TIMES, WORST OF TIMES

Many nonathletes would switch places with famous, highly paid, pro players in a heartbeat, envious of the benefits that come with being squarely in the limelight. It seems the opposite is true as well, since the rich and famous yearn for more privacy and an escape from the constant media scrutiny. Many athletes and coaches never get a firm grasp on the fact that with the good—the large salaries and exotic lifestyle—comes hefty challenges, like having to answer questions following failures on and off the field of play.

But it's not all glamour and glory. There are athletes and pro teams we can only feel sorry for, because their status as lovable losers—hello, Chicago Cubs—leads to jab after jab. Consequently, some of those old comedic standbys, such as football linemen and the Los Angeles Clippers, end up as the butt of repeated jokes.

YOU DON'T SAY!

Usually when I wake up in the middle of the night, it's to do something else.

—2005 Masters champion Tiger Woods, when asked if he ever wakes up at night and finds himself amazed at what he has accomplished in golf

OK, now, everyone together: "Gentlemen, start your interns!"

—Bill Scheft of *Sports Illustrated*, on former U.S. president Bill Clinton announcing he will attend the Indianapolis 500

Madonna announced that she's four months pregnant. I wonder who the lucky team is. I believe the father is the Denver Nuggets.

—*Tonight Show* host Jay Leno

The entire Eastern Conference of the NBA issued "no comment."

—Comedian Alex Kaseberg, after Madonna announced she is pregnant again

It's $19.95, assault and battery not included.

—David Letterman, on the new Dennis Rodman doll

Sadly, America's oldest man has died at age 114. However, Don King is confident that he'll be able to find another opponent for George Foreman.

—Bob Lacey, *Half Moon Bay (CA) Review*

When we started, it was based on lies. It's changing now. There are no secrets in the business. You've got to come with the truth, the whole truth, and nothing but the truth. It's becoming very confusing.

—Promoter Don King,
on boxing's ranking system

What does the Magic P.A. announcer say at halftime to get the crowd going? "Please drive carefully."

—Comedian Alan Ray, on the Orlando Magic following a 19-game losing streak

Randy Moss [of the Oakland Raiders] has already called in sick.

—Scott Ostler of the *San Francisco Chronicle*, pointing out that March 1 is National Sportsmanship Day

What impressed me most is that Webb's time was a full two seconds faster than Barry Bonds' home-run trot.

—Scott Ostler, after Allan Webb ran the mile in a record of 3:53:43

Look, another satisfied customer.

—NHL superstar Brett Hull, after he noticed a fan asleep at a league game

Reporters begged him to make it two.

—Richard Justice of aol.com, on the reaction to manager Buck Showalter's plan to ban the media from watching the first hour of Texas Rangers workouts each day

Finally, the Brewers have figured a way to get a "W" on opening day.

—Comedian Jerry Perisho, after the Milwaukee Brewers announced that President Bush will throw out the first pitch at Milwaukee's new stadium

The worst part was that I thought I heard a couple of guys on my team saying, "Let her take it."

—Chicago White Sox first baseman Paul Konerko, after a young girl with a glove joined him on the warning track in chasing a foul pop-up by Chuck Knoblauch

If Britain really wanted to punish Iraq, it should have sent its 4,000 soccer fans.

—Angus Jones, satirist, on Britain's decision to send troops to the Persian Gulf

Apparently, the U.S. State Department is trying to determine if their bows and arrows qualify as weapons of mass destruction.

—Gavin McDougald of couchmaster.ca, on the Iraqi archers who can't get clearance to compete in the world championships in New York

Paying full price for a [Los Angeles] Clippers ticket—that is March Madness.

—Los Angeles comic Jenny Church, on the NCAA basketball tournament

October 31 is the night people dress in bizarre, outlandish outfits and then make children and old people scream in horror. In most of the world, this is known as Halloween. In Southern California, it is the start of the Clippers' season.

—Comedian Jerry Perisho

They assumed he was smashed out of his mind, because he allegedly was at a bar saying that he would love to play for the Clippers.

—Comedy writer Alex Kaseberg, after Dennis Rodman was arrested in Newport Beach on suspicion of public intoxication

The L.A. Clippers picked high school star Darius Miles with their first choice in the NBA draft. That's the equivalent of being voted off the island.

—Alex Kaseberg

I don't like Chinese food.

—L.A. Clippers forward Bobby Simpson, before his team's early season trip to Tokyo

A pooch named Gaelforce Post Script became the first Scottish terrier since 1965 to win best-in-show at the Westminster Kennel Club. Benoit Benjamin finished a close second.

—Bob Kravitz of the *Rocky Mountain News*, making reference to a former Clipper

Winning.

—Los Angeles Lakers center Shaquille O'Neal, on what he missed most about not coming back to Vancouver since the Grizzlies left for Memphis

Oklahoma State Penitentiary guards cut into an exercise yard basketball and found two pounds of marijuana. They had no idea it was an official NBA ball.

—Comedian and broadcaster Jim Barach

That makes sense. Isn't he part of the Lakers' supporting cast?

—Lisa Dillman of the *Los Angeles Times*, after L.A. Lakers guard Derek Fisher commissioned Victoria's Secret to make him a designer bra in team colors to auction off for charity

That should be about as effective as rotating the Firestone tires on an Explorer.

—Comedian Alex Kaseberg, after the San Diego Chargers announced they would play two quarterbacks, Jim Harbaugh and Moses Moreno, in the first half against the Bills

Now available . . . A rare autographed photo of Terrell Owens. It's rare not because it's signed with the receiver's infamous Sharpie, it's rare because in the photograph, his mouth is almost closed.

—Scott Feschuk of the *National (Toronto) Post*, on a Christmas gift suggestion

Confident.

—Terrell Owens of the Philadelphia Eagles, when asked for one word to describe himself. Then, when asked for another word, he said: "Very."

IT'S THE FIRST TIME I'VE EVER BEEN USED FOR LONG RELIEF.

—Dave Smith, Houston Astros reliever, after a visit to Shea Stadium, where a Mets fan urinated on him as he sat in the bullpen

Prom night was one of the worst nights of my life. My girlfriend looked fantastic . . . The problem was, so did her date.

—Baltimore Ravens' Deion Sanders, recalling his high school days

That's like saying he's the best downhill skier in the Bahamas.

—Josh Lewin of Fox Sports, on the Cleveland Indians dominance, which has been confined to the AL Central

A surefire way for baseball to avert a strike? Bring in Rick Ankiel.

—Larry Stone of the *Seattle Times*, mixing baseball's labor woes with a control-challenged pitcher

But I'm only thirty-two in the Dominican Republic.

—Forty-two-year-old Florida outfielder Tim Raines, on his age

Never forget that all records are made to be broken, especially "Who Let the Dogs Out?"

—*Rocky Mountain News* columnist Bernie Lincicome

He still walks him.

—From *The Sporting News*, after Chicago White Sox pitcher Kip Wells named his new dog "First Pitch Strike"

I once scouted a pitcher who was so bad that when he came into a game the grounds crew dragged the warning track.

—Chicago White Sox scout Fred Smith

A heckuva lot better than being the shortest player in the minor leagues.

—Five-foot-four Freddie Patek, when a member of the Kansas City Royals asked how it felt to be the shortest player in the major leagues

You have to give Pete credit for what he accomplished. He never went to college, and the only book he ever read was the *Pete Rose Story*.

—Pete Rose's ex-wife, Karolyn Rose

It was too bad I wasn't a second baseman, then I'd probably have seen a lot more of my husband.

—Karolyn Rose

Your children boo you at home . . . Your dog gives you a "high rear leg" instead of a "high-five," and you go to a confession and the priest says: "Don't bother . . . I saw your last game."

—Jerry Greene of the *Orlando Sentinel*, on signs why you may be a Tampa Bay Devil Ray

The Yankees made headlines when it was revealed they are forcing Orlando Hernandez to speak English. The Red Sox followed suit by forcing Rickey Henderson to also speak English.

—Matt Crossman in the *Sporting News*

Perhaps the problem with our ozone layer is that Rickey's ego keeps punching holes in it.

—Sean Horgan, the *Hartford Courant* baseball writer, after Rickey Henderson announced, "I am the greatest," following his 939th stolen base

The other day I watched the Rockies taking batting practice and the pitching machine threw a no-hitter.

—Colorado Rockies radio announcer Pete Jones

There's nothing in the world I wouldn't do for Walter O'Malley. There's nothing he wouldn't do for me. That's the way it is. We go through life doing nothing for each other.

—Gene Autry, when he owned the Angels

The first 1,500 fans at tomorrow's Pacific Coast League game in Tacoma will receive Gaylord Perry bobblehead dolls, believed to be the first bobbles in history that can double as Vaseline dispensers.

—Dwight Perry of the *Seattle Times*

It's a hard slider.

—Allison Perry, five-year-old daughter of pitcher Gaylord Perry, when asked if her daddy threw a grease ball

They were all smiles around the state of Minnesota—and in six or seven homes in the Montreal area.

—Fox's Steve Lyons, on baseball's postponement of its contraction plan

You would have a Neil Diamond hit.

—Bud Geracie of the *San Jose Mercury News*, describing what you have if you cross Montreal Expos minor-leaguer Seung Song with Vida Blue

Roger Clemens going into the Hall of Fame as a New York Yankee is like George Harrison going into the Rock and Roll Hall of Fame as a Traveling Wilbury.

—Mike Bianchi of the *Orlando Sentinel*

I haven't seen a guy this happy to leave New York since *Green Acres* was playing in prime time.

—Jim Armstrong of the *Denver Post*, after the New York Mets traded second baseman Roberto Alomar to the Chicago White Sox

YOU DON'T SAY!

In a city that never sleeps, he did.

—*Newsday*, on Roberto Alomar's unhappy year and a half with the Mets

If you eliminated all the jerks from the Hall, it would be as crowded as the ethics room at Enron.

—Rick Telander of the *Chicago Sun-Times*, on character as a criteria for induction into the Baseball Hall of Fame

Raise the urinals.

—Ex-major-league infielder Darrel Chaney, on how management could keep the Braves on their toes

As a visiting team, you love it when the guy comes on and says, "Show me the monkey!"

—Minnesota Twins catcher A. J. Pierzynski, talking about the Anaheim Angels' rally monkey

That "rally monkey" looks an awful lot like the guy in charge of the Cincinnati Bengals' personnel decisions.

—Mike Bianchi of the *Orlando Sentinel,* after another non-playoff season in Cincinnati

The action scenes in *Remember the Titans* were performed by actors with little football training. For many of the shots, they used the Cincinnati Bengals.

—Comedy writer Alan Ray

RAIDER DEFENSIVE TACKLE DARRELL RUSSELL HAS BEEN SUSPENDED FOR A YEAR AFTER TESTING POSITIVE FOR ECSTASY. IN A RELATED STORY, THE DETROIT LIONS' ENTIRE TEAM RECENTLY TESTED POSITIVE FOR AGONY.

—Jim Armstrong of the *Denver Post*

It's a lonesome walk to the sidelines, especially when thousands of people are cheering your replacement.

—Minnesota Vikings quarterback Fran Tarkenton

They're going to make a movie starring Denzel Washington out of Tennessee's 24–10 loss to the Baltimore Ravens . . . It will be called *Dismember the Titans*.

—Comedy writer Alex Kaseberg

New Orleans mayor opens Superdome as hurricane shelter. Refugees defeat Saints 42–6.

—Headline from fark.com

Midwestern farmers are now using equipment that turns manure into energy. You know, the reverse of the Bears.

—Steve Rosenbloom of the *Chicago Tribune*, on the woeful Bears, in the midst of an eight-game losing streak

He's the only NFL player to end up on *Sportscenter* and ESPN Classic the same day.

—ESPN analyst Sterling Sharpe, on aging Carolina Panthers quarterback Rodney Peete

Peyton Manning's request to wear black high-tops as a tribute to the late Johnny Unitas was denied by the NFL, but the Indy quarterback ended up getting fined anyway after the league ruled he tossed up all those interceptions against Miami as a tribute to Ryan Leaf.

—Scott Feschuk of the *National (Toronto) Post*

"Where they gonna build it?" Barkley asked. Said Woods, "In the space between your ball and mine."

—The *Houston Chronicle*, on a round of golf in Las Vegas as Tiger Woods asked Charles Barkley if he had heard about the new Super Kmart store being built in that city

Just out of curiosity, now that I've come out of my so-called slump, am I the leading candidate for Comeback Player of the Year?

—Tiger Woods, after winning the Western Open with a record-tying score of 21-under par

I can just hear Elin now: "Honey, I sold that ugly green jacket at the garage sale. Some nice man named Mickelson picked it up for $5."

—Mike Bianchi of the *Orlando Sentinel*, in the days before Phil Mickelson ended his major tournament drought, envisioning Tiger Woods' life as a newlywed

It's once again apparent Mickelson will never be a Tiger.

—Larry Stewart of the *Los Angeles Times*, on Detroit's Toledo farm team declining to sign golfer/pitcher Phil Mickelson

Grass isn't his best surface.

—NBC golf analyst Roger Maltbie, after watching former tennis great Ivan Lendl hit five balls into a water hazard on the eighteenth hole of a celebrity golf tournament

That putt was so good I could feel the baby applaud.

—Golfer Donna Horton-White, after making a twenty-five-foot putt while seven months pregnant

I mean, the only thing missing was Happy Gilmore.

—*Vancouver Province* columnist Ed Willes, on the seventy-second hole of the U.S. Open where Retief Goosen missed a two-foot putt for the win and earlier Mark Brooks bogeyed the hole and Stewart Cink double-bogeyed

The only reason I don't like playing in the World Series is I can't watch myself play.

—Former major-league slugger Reggie Jackson

As long as he keeps that fastball above the belt, I could stand there until I get my pension and still be another notch on his gun.

—Reggie Jackson, on pitcher Roger Clemens

YOU DON'T SAY!

What's everyone blaming me for? Blame Felix. I wouldn't have hit into the double plays if he hadn't hit singles.

—Joe Torre, while playing for the New York Mets, after tying a major-league record by hitting into four double plays, each time after Felix Millan had singled just before Torre came to the plate

The Cubs went over 2.1 million Sunday. But enough about games behind.

—Steve Rosenbloom of the *Chicago Tribune*

Today I told my little girl I was going to the ballpark. And she asked, "What for?"

—L.A. Dodgers utility man Dave Anderson, on the joys of never playing

I was afraid I was going to die. Then, I played for the Seattle Mariners, and I was sure I was going to die.

—Former major-league player Glenn Wilson, on his heart murmur

George Steinbrenner hopes to have a new Yankee Stadium ready by 2009. It will be "The House That Ruthless Built."

—Bill Littlejohn, in Tom FitzGerald's syndicated column

Nothing's more limited than being a limited partner of George's.

—John McMullen, Astros owner, on his former limited partner George Steinbrenner

You know you're in trouble when you're fielding your own wild pitches.

—Baltimore Orioles pitcher Gregg Olson, after tossing three wild pitches in one inning, two of which caromed toward first base

I told him I wasn't tired. He told me, "No, but our outfielders sure are."

—Former Texas Rangers pitcher Jim Kern, recalling a time he was removed from a game by his manager

Six in the city.

—Headline on mlb.com, after six Houston Astros pitchers combined on a no-hitter at Yankee Stadium

I was like, "Ha-ha, he hit a car!" And then I found out it was mine and it wasn't so funny.

—New York Mets outfielder Karim Garcia, after teammate José Reyes' batting-practice foul broke a window in a Hummer in the players' parking lot

Willie Mays, in his late thirties, makes a fantastic catch. On the radio, Russ Hodges says, "That Mays is amazing. He has the body of a twenty-year-old." Simmons follows, "I had the body of a twenty-year-old last night, but my wife found out about it."

—Former San Francisco Giants and Oakland A's broadcaster Lon Simmons, recalling this baseball gem

I went through life as a "player to be named later."

—Joe Garagiola, former catcher, on his major-league career

The bad news: The game is in Puerto Rico.

—Cam Hutchinson of the *Saskatoon StarPhoenix*, on the news that the Blue Jays and Expos will play their traditional Canada Day game on July 2

That infamous foul ball that Cubs fan Steve Bartman deflected away from left fielder Moises Alou in the National League playoffs goes up for auction, with bids starting at $5,000. The winning price, we assume, includes shipping and mishandling fees.

—Dwight Perry of the *Seattle Times*

Now the only way the Red Sox can get rid of him is if they trade him and agree to assume 80 percent of his attitude.

—Bill Scheft of *Sports Illustrated*, after moody Boston slugger Manny Ramirez cleared irrevocable waivers

Experts believe this will increase home runs by fifty to fifty-two if you count homers by the Tigers.

—Bill Scheft, on Detroit moving its fence in left-center field twenty-five feet closer to home plate

Chuck—you wish you threw like a girl.

—A sign greeting Yankees left fielder Chuck Knoblauch in Minneapolis referred to his throwing problems that cost him his second-base spot

It's always been a tough park for hitters.

—Dick Schaap, ABC commentator, after watching a wrecking ball crash into old Comiskey Park in Chicago but fail to do any damage

Just wondering: With the College World Series title going to Rice, does that make them the Boys of Simmer?

—Dwight Perry of the *Seattle Times*

OK, it's David, but we're still betting he votes down any invite from the Alamo Bowl.

—Dwight Perry, on Arizona cornerback Davey Crockett

If they tell Jim McMahon we have a ten o'clock curfew, he'll probably think that means 10 A.M. the next day.

—Chicago Bears tackle Dan Hampton, on Super Bowl week

Our defensive backs were like a river. There was a lot more activity at the mouth than at the source.

—Cleveland Browns center Mike Baab, on his team's defensive backfield

He's like the big brother I never wanted.

—Howie Long, on fellow Fox Sports analyst Terry Bradshaw

His receivers were on the second floor.

—NFL great Johnny Unitas, after it was reported that Oakland quarterback Dan Pastorini had thrown a football from a hotel parking lot up to a sixth-floor balcony

If Clark had played the way he judged talent, that ball he caught against the Cowboys would now be known as "The Drop."

—Bill Livingston of the *Cleveland Plain Dealer*, on ex-49ers receiver Dwight Clark's tenure as a Cleveland Browns vice president

We promised we'd trim our roster. So we cut a continent and signed a country.

—Winnipeg Blue Bombers spokesman Shawn Coates, after the team released safety Tom Europe and signed D-lineman Tom Canada

Alert statisticians have discovered that Namath, who retired in 1967, just broke the NFL record for the most seasons between incomplete passes.

—Dwight Perry of the *Seattle Times,* after Joe Namath, the ex-Jets quarterback whose sideline interview was cut short because he twice told ESPN's Suzy Kolber, "I want to kiss you"

Who Wants to Kiss Joe Namath?

—Cam Hutchinson of the *Saskatoon StarPhoenix*, on the name of Fox's next reality television series

Latest XFL innovation: Fifteen-yard penalty for excessive sportsmanship.

—Jim Armstrong of the *Denver Post*

The XFL, we're told, is actually a Roman numeral. It stands for "Ten Fans Left."

—Phil Mushnick of the *New York Post*

This calls for a measurement.

—Columnist Scott Ostler, predicting the most often-used phrase from TV announcers during the Lingerie Bowl

Millions of Americans will sit down for a holiday turkey and then, after the Green Bay–Detroit game, they'll eat dinner.

—Janice Hough in the *San Francisco Chronicle*, on the typical Thanksgiving celebration

He certainly adds some intelligence to the profession. When Terry Bradshaw was in high school, he nearly froze to death at the drive-in movie waiting to see *Closed for the Winter.*

—Comedian Argus Hamilton, on Rush Limbaugh joining ESPN's Sunday *NFL Countdown* show

You don't hesitate with Michael or you'll end up on some poster in a gift shop somewhere.

—Felton Spencer of the Minnesota Timberwolves, on guarding Michael Jordan

I'm often mentioned in the same sentence as Michael Jordan. You know—that Scott Hastings, he's no Michael Jordan.

—Denver Nuggets backup center Scott Hastings

Maybe he really is the next Jordan.

—Tom FitzGerald of the *San Francisco Chronicle*, after LeBron James took in a little batting practice before a Reds-Indians game in Cleveland—and swung and missed at the first nine BP pitches he saw

YOU DON'T SAY!

Now I know how Fred Roberts feels every time he takes a jump shot.

—Boston's Larry Bird, after making only four of nineteen shots

If we were looking for citizenship, we'd disband the league.

—Minnesota Timberwolves executive Kevin McHale, on what scouts do not search for in the NBA draft

I call myself Ted Williams. They've had me frozen solid for the last six months and thawed me out for this.

—San Antonio guard Steve Kerr, who, at age thirty-seven, came off the Spurs bench to fuel a comeback victory over the Dallas Mavericks in Game 6 of the NBA Western Conference Final

Clark Kent went into the phone booth and came out as Lois Lane.

—Sportswriter Jack McCallum, on Laker Kurt Rambis' mediocore play in the playoffs

HOUSTON ROCKETS NO. 1 PICK YAO MING HAS SOMETHING IN COMMON WITH MOST AMERICANS. HE'LL NEED AN INTERPRETER WHEN HE GOES TO TEXAS.

—Bob Molinaro of the *Norfolk Virginian-Pilot*

I really lack the words to compliment myself today.

—Skiing great Alberto Tomba

Are they nuts? MLS adding multiple franchises is the equivalent of Ford announcing a new line of Pintos.

—Syndicated columnist Norman Chad, on Major League Soccer planning to expand by two teams

Hey ref, if you had another eye, you'd be a Cyclops.

—Frustrated Italian soccer fan yelling at a referee

I knew something was wrong when I came to a locked gate.

—American racewalker Ron Laird, after he went off course in the 20,000-meter walk championships

Just what does a person have to do in figure skating to be banned for life? Wear bib overalls to the long program? Or maybe, slip some Slim Whitman into a competitor's music?

—Steve Hummer of the *Atlanta Journal-Constitution*, on figure skating suspensions

Do you have any other problems, other than that you're unemployed and a moron and a dork?

—Tennis great John McEnroe, to a spectator who annoyed him

The scary part for Americans is not that Steffi Graf, Michael Stitch, and Boris Becker are playing better tennis than any Yank players, but that they also speak better English than most.

—*New York Times* columnist George Vecsey, after Germans dominated at Wimbledon

Suggested nickname for this squad: "The Little Engine That Could."

—Tom FitzGerald of the *San Francisco Chronicle*, on Harvard's tennis team which includes Chris Chiou, Jonathan Chu, and Oliver Choo

Headline writers, we hear, are flooding psychiatry hotlines after experiencing the same recurring nightmare, in which Mark Calcavecchia announces he is engaged to fellow golfer Virada Nirapathpongporn. And the sequels only get worse: They've decided to hyphenate.

—Dwight Perry of the *Seattle Times*

Lost: Golfing husband and dog—last seen at Ratliff Ranch Golf Links. Reward for dog.

—Newspaper ad from a golfing widow in Midland, Texas, who's had it with her husband's love of the game

Great trade.

—LPGA Hall of Famer Patty Berg, to a man who said he had gotten a new driver for his wife

I think I'm going to change my name from Juan to nine-Juan-Juan. I'm like the rescue squad. Whenever someone needs help, they call for me.

—Golfer Chi Chi Rodriguez, on his role as a goodwill ambassador for the sport

They call it golf because all of the other four-letter words were taken.

—Golfer Ray Floyd

It's so bad, I could putt off a tabletop and still leave the ball halfway down the leg.

—J. C. Snead, pro golfer, on his putting problems

Walk to the clubhouse holding a one-iron over your head. Not even the good Lord can hit a one-iron.

—Lee Trevino, who was once struck by lightning while playing golf, offering advice on how others can avoid a similar fate

If I had an opportunity to play with a trio of outstanding individuals, but wanted to still have some fun and turn in a decent scorecard, I'd pick George Shearing, Ray Charles, and Stevie Wonder.

—In his *Stupid Little Golf Book*, actor/comedian Leslie Nielsen described his ideal foursome

Congress.

—Former U.S. president Ronald Reagan, in the new golf book, *First Off the Tee*, when asked what his handicap was

I would like to deny all allegations by Bob Hope that during my last game of golf, I hit an eagle, a birdie, an elk, and a moose.

—Former U.S. president Gerald Ford

Anything I want it to be. For instance, this hole right here is a par-47, and yesterday I birdied the sucker.

—Willie Nelson, country music singer, when he was asked what par was on a golf course he'd just purchased

Jeez, the Devils even win show-and-tell.

—Steve Rosenbloom of the *Chicago Tribune*, after learning New Jersey forward Jim McKenzie let his kids take the Stanley Cup to elementary school

It's sort of like your ex saying what a great guy you are as she drives off in the Porsche you're still paying for.

—Gord McIntyre of the *Vancouver Province*, after Scotty Bowman, Brett Hull, and Chris Chelios all praised the Canucks for their play against the Red Wings in the NHL playoffs

It was like taking your wife out to the best dinner you've ever had, followed by the best show at the theater you've ever seen, and then you get back to the car you've got a flat tire.

—Vancouver Canucks general manager Brian Burke, summarizing his team's season following a Game 7 loss to the Minnesota Wild in the second round of the NHL playoffs

If the Preds have a sense for marketing, they should now make a pitch for Canuck draft pick Matt Violin.

—Elliot Pap of the *Vancouver Sun*, after the Nashville Predators called up Vern Fiddler from their Milwaukee AHL farm club

Bumped into Mike Keenan in the elevator the other day. I said to him: "Where ya' going? The basement?"

—Ex-NHL great Dennis Hull, speaking about an NHL coach at a sports legacy dinner to benefit Vancouver's Jewish community center

"Hey, Bronco, there's a fly on the end of your nose." To which Horvath replied: "You get it . . . you're closer to it than me."

—Former Vancouver Canucks general manager Bud Poile, reminiscing about a player he once signed in Edmonton, Bronco Horvath, who was famous for his extremely large Ukrainian nose. Poile related how he ran into Horvath one morning in the lobby of the team's hotel.

I didn't know whether to check him or ask for his autograph.

—Bill Houlder, recalling his first shift in the NHL when he had to check Wayne Gretzky

I just hope I don't end up with my index finger in the air when I try to move my thumb.

—Donald Audette of the Montreal Canadiens, on the delicate surgery needed to repair severed tendons in his arm

YOU DON'T SAY!

The Bruins' problems at left wing continue.

—Sportswriter Dick Trust, after the left wing of the plane carrying the Boston Bruins hit a bus in a minor accident at Los Angeles International Airport

Me, on instant replay.

—Derek Sanderson, when playing for the Boston Bruins, on the best hockey player he ever saw

A logo without a team.

—*Boston Globe* columnist Kevin Dupont, on the San Jose Sharks when they were a sad sack team

If they were faked, you would see me in more of them.

—Rod Gilbert, while playing for the New York Rangers, when asked if hockey fights are faked

Because of a phone call. The one I never got.

—Hockey Hall of Famer Gordie Howe, on why he never coached in the NHL

He shot it right in my jock strap, so it was a good break for me.

—Chicago Blackhawks goalie Jocelyn Thibault, on how he stopped Detroit's Sergei Fedorov on a breakaway

I guess this signifies that the Brass passed Gasse.

—Columnist Doug Kelly, after reading the transaction listing from the East Coast Hockey League that the New Orleans Brass waived goalie Pascal Gasse

A fifteen-year-old female patient yawned continuously for a period of five weeks. This feat was considered all the more remarkable since there is no record of her being a St. Louis Blues season ticket holder.

—Jay Greenberg in the *Hockey News*

The only bad thing about being released by the Senators is they made me keep my season tickets.

—Ex-Ottawa Senators forward Doug Smail

Only one has a spout that can be turned off.

—Randy Turner of the *Winnipeg Free Press*, on the differences between NHL commentator Don Cherry and the mini-beer kegs that bear his suits' likeness

Who's her stylist, Bryan Marchment?

—James Duthie of the Sports Network (Canada), on Canadian curling champ Colleen Jones straining neck ligaments while, among other things, getting her hair done

Let's call it *I'm Going to Make You My Bachelorette*.

—Steve Hummer of the *Atlanta Journal-Constitution*, suggesting the title for a Mike Tyson reality television show

Yesterday I was lying, today I am telling the truth.

—Boxing promoter Bob Arum, replying to a reporter's question

His greatest dream is to die in his own arms.

—Fight promoter Irving Rudd, on boxer Hector "Macho" Camacho

I'd love to be a procrastinator, but I never seem to get around to it.

—Fight promoter Chris Dundee

I put my suitcase down, looked up at the Sears Tower, and said, "Chicago, I'm going to conquer you." When I looked down, my suitcase was gone.

—Boxer James "Quick" Tillis, on his first day in Chicago

Stewardess: "Mr. Ali, please fasten your seat belt."
Ali: "Superman don't need no seat belt."
Stewardess: "Superman don't need no airplane, either."

—Former heavyweight boxing champ Muhammad Ali, losing a battle of wits with an Eastern Airlines flight attendant

CHAPTER 2

A LOVELY RUSSIAN LASS NAMED ANNA

Anna Kournikova was a very good tennis player—when she was the top-rated junior in the world. Since turning pro, however, Kournikova has become the best-known female athlete on the planet, but not because she was a regular winner on the women's pro tour. In fact, when she opted for an early retirement, it was clearly noted that Anna had not won a WTA event. But tennis isn't the reason Anna became one of the most famous, most photographed, and most downloaded women in the world. No, people talk about Anna because she's just so damn easy to look at.

Let's talk about bras.

—Anna Kournikova, deflecting questions about her love life, at a promotional event for her new line of sportswear

The one drawback, of course, is that it looks a lot better than it performs.

—Michael Ventre of msnbc.com, on the new "Anna Bra"

Apparently Kournikova's people examined the photo closely and spotted a first-place trophy in the background.

—Michael Ventre, on how the fake topless photos of Anna Kournikova in *Penthouse* were found to be false

So Anna Kournikova is suing *Penthouse* magazine, claiming those topless pictures weren't actually her. Can't you wait until this case goes to trial and we get to see Exhibits A and B?

—Jeff Gordon of the *St. Louis Post-Dispatch*

No word yet if Kournikova will sue, but it would be the only court appearance she'd actually have a good chance of winning.

—Ken Rudolph of Fox Sports, on the report that unauthorized nude pictures of Anna Kournikova will appear in *Penthouse* magazine

British men's magazine *FHM* named Anna Kournikova the "Sexiest Woman in the World." Let's just hope they were looking at the right photos.

—Comedian Jerry Perisho

Hey, Anna, any chance of a little glimpse into the future?

—Sean Callahan in the *San Francisco Chronicle*, after Kournikova told *Inside Tennis* that in the future, female tennis players will be competing topless

Kournikova's parents like their legal chances in this case, given their daughter has never scored a major court victory.

—Chris Dufresne of the *Los Angeles Times*, after Anna Kournikova's parents sued her for allegedly taking over the Miami Beach waterfront home the three jointly own

The only thing faster in women's tennis than Venus Williams' serve is Anna Kournikova's exit.

—Comedian Alan Ray

Trading away the rights to Michael Vick just because you had a bad time with Ryan Leaf is like turning down a date with Anna Kournikova because you got slapped around a bit by Tonya Harding.

—Columnist Scott Ostler, after the San Diego Chargers passed on quarterback Michael Vick in the NFL draft partly because they'd been burned by the Ryan Leaf experience

Today in the Australian Open, Anna Kournikova double-faulted twice and had twenty-nine unforced errors in her defeat, or, as she calls it, being in the zone.

—Late-night talk show host Craig Kilborn

Anna Kournikova says that she may retire from the sport of tennis. This is bad news to the player who was rated second to last in the world.

—Craig Kilborn

In a major upset, softball player Jennie Finch unseated defending champ Anna Kournikova as the hottest female athlete in an espn.com poll. That's unfortunate, because this has been our only chance to call Kournikova a defending champion.

—Jay Leno

Tabloids are reporting that Jaden Gil, the twenty-one-month-old son of Andre Agassi and Steffi Graf, has already begun taking tennis lessons. And over the weekend, he beat Anna Kournikova.

—Jay Leno

WHEN ANNA KOURNIKOVA WED ENRIQUE IGLESIAS RECENTLY, SHE HAD ALL THE TRADITIONAL TRAPPINGS. THE "SOMETHING BORROWED" WAS A TENNIS TROPHY.

—Comedy writer Alan Ray

Isn't that like learning how to play football from the Cincinnati Bengals?

—*Tonight Show* host Jay Leno, after *People* reported that Kournikova is giving Enrique Iglesias tennis lessons

In a twist of irony, we should note that Kournikova previously had serious romantic trysts with NHL stars Sergei Fedorov and Pavel Bure—at least before she locked them out.

—Randy Turner of the *Winnipeg Free Press*, on Anna Kournikova tying the knot with singer Enrique Iglesias

You can see his point of view. He asks her where she was all day, and she says: "Practicing tennis" . . . then he sees her play.

—Jay Leno, after hockey star Sergei Fedorov said news reports of Kournikova seeing other men sabotaged their short-lived marriage

Now that Pavel Bure and Anna Kournikova have broken up, I expect Sergei Fedorov's play to pick up.

—Mark Kriegel of the *New York Daily News*

In the old days, the Russian players would have been sent to Siberia . . . Now they have a one-month ban on dating Anna Kournikova.

—Steve Abney in the *San Francisco Chronicle*, after host Russia failed to qualify for the quarterfinals at the World Hockey Championship in St. Petersburg

I don't know if Anna told him to get tougher or what.

—Stars center Mike Modano, on Sergei Fedorov breaking three sticks on Dallas players

I'm a hockey player.

—A male fan's sign directed at Kournikova at the Bank of the West Classic in Stanford

Sergei Fedorov for Paul Kariya? I make that switch if I'm the Anaheim Mighty Ducks, especially if there's an ex-girlfriend to be named later.

—Cam Hutchinson of the *Saskatoon StarPhoenix*, on the NHL's roster shuffling

The younger guys in our office seem to know just a little too much about twenty-year-old Russian tennis sensation Daniela Hantuchova. I guess I'm old school. I like Anna.

—Cam Hutchinson

John McEnroe reports that Anna Kournikova lost her opening-round match at Wimbledon because, among other things, "she is not in very good shape." All I can say is thank goodness he hasn't seen the women I've been dating.

—Jim Greene in the *San Francisco Chronicle*

Isn't banning a team that finished 1–10 last year from playing in a bowl game similar to telling Anna Kournikova she's ineligible to play in the Wimbledon final?

—Dwight Perry of the *Seattle Times*, on the University of California football team being banned from NCAA bowl consideration

Reaction was swift. Roger Federer, oddsmakers' morning-line favorite to be on center court for Sunday's final, has been replaced by Anna Kournikova.

—Dwight Perry, after Madrid Masters tennis organizers sacked the traditional ballboys and ballgirls and replaced them with glamorous female models

Both are beautiful blond Russians. The only difference is that Kournikova never liked working weekends.

—Comedian and broadcaster Jim Barach, on 2004 Wimbledon champion Maria Sharapova being compared to Kournikova

I'm not the next Kournikova—I want to win matches!

—Maria Sharapova, downplaying comparisons between her and another Russian

CHAPTER 3

FREUDIAN QUIPS

Sex sells! It also creeps into the minds of professional athletes both on and off the field. The NBA's troubles with players fathering out-of-wedlock children allowed columnists and commentators to have a field day, but basketball isn't the only culprit. Thanks in part to Boris Becker's short rally with a model in a London restaurant, tennis has now taken "love" to a whole new level.

My cleavage.

—Mountain bike gold medalist Paola Pezzo of Italy, when asked what she is most famous for back home

I'm surprised the president didn't offer to share the suite with her.

—Rex Stults of KVYN-FM in Napa, California, after Martina Hingis, who was playing in the German Open, got bumped from the presidential suite at the Intercontinental Hotel in Berlin to make room for President Clinton

The worst lie since "I didn't have sex with that woman, Miss Lewinsky."

—Vancouver, B.C., broadcaster Brad Fay, repeating a one-liner comparing an awkward ball-striking position at the U.S. Open with an infamous moment in U.S. presidential history

Yeah. I do. But it's sure better than being known as her current husband.

—Tom Arnold of Fox Sports Net's *Best Damn Sports Show Period*, after *Newsweek* asked him, "Do you worry that you'll always be known as Roseanne's ex-husband?"

The nation's hot spot was Death Valley—104 [degrees]. You know what the nation's cold spot was? The couch Kobe Bryant was sleeping on.

—*Tonight Show* host Jay Leno

It's something like the third-largest diamond ever mined in Russia. They say they're saving it for Kobe's next affair.

—Jay Leno, on miners uncovering a 301-carat diamond

The newest Laker Karl Malone said he joined the team because he wanted to get a ring. So I guess he's hoping that Kobe cheats on him, too.

—Jay Leno, after Kobe bought his wife a $4 million ring as an apology for his adultery

I'm glad that he got off. You never want to see a player of his caliber go down for something like that. Now he can go back to being a family man.

—Shaquille O'Neal, after sexual assault charges against former teammate Kobe Bryant were dropped

Good news for NBA players who can't afford $4 million, eight-karat purple diamond rings.

—Steve Rosenbloom of the *Chicago Tribune*, on Greece licensing more brothels during the 2004 Summer Olympics

This Women of the Olympics feature will remind readers that world-class athletes take off their pants one leg at a time, just like normal people.

—Jeff Gordon of the *St. Louis Post-Dispatch*, after eight U.S. Olympians were featured in *Playboy*

The Storm had no official stance, other than to mention that plenty of good seats are available.

—Jerry Greene of the *Orlando Sentinel*, after Seattle Storm WNBA star Lauren Jackson posed nude for an Australian magazine

This is a double disaster, because the last thing anyone wants to see is Irina Korzhanenko stripped.

—Gavin McDougald of couchmaster.ca, after a Russian shot-putter was stripped of her Olympic gold medal for failing a drug test

The only thing missing from their "uniforms" were the garter belts stuffed with dollar bills.

—Mike Bianchi of the *Orlando Sentinel*, on the skimpy beach-volleyball outfits that were worn during the Summer Olympics

It was reported that 836,000 condoms were handed out at the Sydney Olympics in 2000. And that was just to the U.S. men's basketball team.

—Cam Hutchinson, *Saskatoon StarPhoenix*

My roommate from Algeria checked in at 1:30 A.M. and began praying while watching porn. True story. I told him he had to pick one or the other.

—U.S. Olympic javelin thrower Breaux Greer

Not bad considering [the breast] probably only cost Janet five grand.

—fark.com, after CBS was fined $550,000 by the Federal Communications Commission for showing Janet Jackson's breast during the infamous Super Bowl halftime show

Justin Timberlake called the incident a "wardrobe malfunction." The last time I had one of those, I became a father.

—*Late Show* host David Letterman, on the same Super Bowl halftime entertainment

Janet Jackson and Michael Jackson now make everybody so nervous, don't be surprised if the NFL threatens to take away the 2005 Super Bowl unless the host city, Jacksonville, agrees to change its name.

—Mike Downey of the *Chicago Tribune*

You'd think twenty years after high school you'd be safe from losing your girl to the quarterback.

—Screenwriter Scott Rosenberg, on his ex-girlfriend, model/actress Bridget Moynahan, dating Super Bowl MVP Tom Brady

Are you still the alternative?

—Tennis great Martina Navratilova, to a British tabloid reporter at Wimbledon who asked if she was still a lesbian

She endures a double whammy—while Ivan Lendl suffers for being too little a man and too much a machine, Martina suffers for being too much of both.

—Commentator Bud Collins, on Martina Navratilova's struggle to be accepted by tennis fans

Sources indicate it was an unplanned pregnancy, also known as a "double fault."

—Syndicated columnist Norman Chad, after word leaked out that Andre Agassi and Steffi Graf were expecting a baby

I now interrupt this column—it's a personal rain delay—to present highlights of Bud Collins' commentary on Sunday: 1) "OHHH!" 2) "OOOOH!" 3) "Whew!" 4) "AHHHHHH!" I'm not sure if he was watching tennis or giving birth.

—Norman Chad, on NBC's coverage of Wimbledon

I wore leather. White is for Wimbledon.

—Tennis star Hana Mandlikova, explaining what she wore to her wedding

This is like the Breeders' Cup.

—NBC tennis analyst Mary Carillo, after noticing that John McEnroe has a new baby at home, Tracy Austin recently gave birth to her first, and Chris Evert was expecting her third child

Is that considered a forced or unforced error?

—Michael Ventre of msnbc.com, on Jennifer Capriati throwing a punch at her boyfriend, but hitting a nightclub waitress instead

Every time Venus tossed up to serve, I was thinking, "Oh no, they won't fall out, will they?"

—ESPN's Pam Shriver, on the three-piece, low-cut outfit Venus Williams wore during play at the Australian Open

Just what is the nationality of a child with a Russian mother and German father conceived in a Japanese restaurant in England?

—Dwight Perry of the *Seattle Times*, after Boris Becker admitted to being the father of a ten-month-old girl born to a Russian model

Boris Becker admits to being the father of a ten-month-old girl born to a Russian model. The model, Angela Ermakova, says she met Becker in a London bar and later had sex with him in the closet of a Japanese restaurant. You've got to like a place that offers "an intimate dining experience."

—Tom FitzGerald of the *San Francisco Chronicle*

And I thought his serve was fast.

—Comedian Alex Kaseberg, after a London court approved a financial offer from Boris Becker to support the baby he fathered with a Russian model. Becker said it was an act that lasted just five seconds in a closet

Dennis Rodman and Carmen Electra are calling it quits. Apparently their marriage couldn't withstand the old seven-day itch.

—Alex Kaseberg

In a recent magazine interview, actress Carmen Electra claims she thinks about sex every twenty seconds. That's why she and Dennis Rodman were so incompatible. He operates on a twenty-four-second clock.

—Comedian Jerry Perisho

Max Factor had just died, and Dennis had a tough time getting his game face on.

—Comedian Argus Hamilton, explaining a poor playoff game from Dennis Rodman of the Chicago Bulls

Dennis Rodman played an exhibition game in Puerto Rico for the Isabela Roosters. It's a shame when the once-mighty are humbled and must resort to that, but enough about the Roosters.

—Greg Cote of the *Miami Herald*

I see that Wilt Chamberlain's Philly schoolboy career scoring mark was broken by Maurice Davis. Upon surpassing Wilt's 2,206 points, Davis was mobbed by teammates, students, and 20,001 women.

—Peter Vescey of the *New York Post*

This just in: Wilt Chamberlain wants us to know that absentee ballots have raised the number from 20,000 to 30,000.

—Dave Kindred of the *Sporting News*

Researchers have found that having sex can harm your eyesight. Finally, we know why Wilt Chamberlain was such a terrible free-throw shooter. He couldn't see the rim.

—Comedy writer Jerry Perisho

News item: Lebronjames.com went online Monday, and the Web site attracted more than 3,000 first-day visitors. Sports historians weren't impressed, however, pointing out that 3,000 isn't even halfway to the NBA's twenty-four-hour record for hits—established in 1962 by Wilt Chamberlain at a Philly singles bar.

—Dwight Perry of the *Seattle Times*

Cleveland Cavaliers star Shawn Kemp, who's fathered seven children by six women, may be a great basketball player but he obviously knows nothing about safe sex. What does he think HIV means? High five?

—Bob Lacey, *Half Moon Bay (CA) Review*

According to an organization that charts babies' names, you know the most popular name for a baby girl? Kaitlyn. You know the most popular name for boys? Shawn Kemp Jr.

—Jay Leno

One thing we know about Shawn Kemp: He wasn't sleepless in Seattle.

—*Toronto Sun* columnist Steve Simmons on a former Super Sonic

I just hope my wife was watching this game back at home so she doesn't think I got those scratches someplace else.

—Scott Hastings, Atlanta Hawks forward/center, after a fight with Sidney Green of the Chicago Bulls left some prominent scratches on his neck

In it she says: "I've always believed it was more fun in groups."

—The *Philadelphia Daily News*, after Dr. Ruth Westheimer shot a commercial for the Philadelphia 76ers promoting group sales

Officials attribute it to fewer teen pregnancies, an aging population, and an all-consuming interest in video games by NBA players.

—Steve Rosenbloom of the *Chicago Tribune*, on the U.S. birthrate falling to a record low

Talk about making a late-season push.

—Eliott Harris of the *Chicago Sun-Times*, after Arizona State women's basketball coach Charli Turner Thorne delivered a baby shortly after her team received an NCAA tournament berth

Here's the weird part. After they had sex, three players burst in the room and poured a bucket of Gatorade over the coach.

—Jay Leno, on the *Sports Illustrated* report that detailed former Alabama coach Mike Price's sex session with two women in his hotel room

Vijay apologized for saying he hopes Annika misses the cut at the 2003 Colonial. He even said he would love one day to personally help her into the traditional green apron.

—Comedian and broadcaster Jim Barach, on Vijay Singh's anti-Annika Sorenstam stance

The *Vancouver Sun* reported that Kaila Mussell, twenty-four, of Chilliwack plans to compete in 100 pro rodeo events this season as the circuit's first woman saddle-bronc rider since 1929. Reaction was swift. Vijay Singh immediately pulled out of this year's Calgary Stampede.

—Dwight Perry, with a Sorenstam-related joke in the *Seattle Times*

I READ TODAY IN THE PAPER THAT THE POPE WAS A SOCCER GOALIE IN HIS YOUTH. APPARENTLY, EVEN AS A YOUNG MAN HE TRIED TO STOP PEOPLE FROM SCORING.

—NBC's Conan O'Brien

Now there will be even less scoring in soccer.

—Dan Quinn of ESPN radio, after referees in the Premier League of English soccer were banned from having sex the night before games, an edict that used to apply only to players

Ever since my wife found it in the glove compartment.

—Golfer Lee Trevino, when asked when he started wearing a corset for his bad back

Sports Illustrated reports there's a golf course in France that is designed like the body of a naked woman. That should speed up the game. Instead of five hours, guys will be done in, like, two minutes now.

—Jay Leno

My neighbor Bob says if you keep telling a woman she's beautiful, she'll overlook all the other lies.

—Sports columnist Joe Falls

Keegan fills Schmeichel's gap with Seaman.

—*Sky Sports* headline, after soccer standout David Seaman decided to quit Arsenal to join up with Kevin Keegan's Manchester United

When the track announcer yelled, "They're off," Funny Cide reportedly cracked, "I know."

—Michael Ventre of msnbc.com, on Funny Cide becoming the first gelding since 1929 to win the Kentucky Derby

A baby finished the Boston Marathon in just under seven hours. His mom, forty-six, who is seven months pregnant, finished a split second later.

—Comedian Jerry Perisho

The joke now is we had too many men on the ice.

—Goalie Sarah Tueting, on teammate Lisa Brown-Miller, who played on the U.S. women's Olympic hockey team in Nagano, Japan, even though it was discovered afterward that she was pregnant during the run for the gold medal (she gave birth to a boy six months after the Olympics)

Things already look promising for three-day-old Tim Montgomery, son of world sprint champions Tim Montgomery and Marion Jones. Turns out that, no matter how many Legos or Tinker Toys they put in his bassinet, the kid only wants to stare at his starting blocks.

—Dwight Perry of the *Seattle Times*

Congratulations to sprinters Tim Montgomery and Marion Jones on the speedy and safe arrival of their baby. To be honest, I always like it when Montgomery is in the news. "See, hon," I say to my wife, "I am not the fastest man in the world."

—Cam Hutchinson of the *Saskatoon StarPhoenix*

Was I nervous? Does Dolly Parton sleep on her back?

—Jockey Chris McCarron, on how he felt before taking Alysheba to the post in the Preakness

I do a lot of comedy, and some dancing. I can't say I sing . . . when I sing, people think the place is being raided.

—Morganna "Kissing Bandit" Roberts, on her nightclub act

Best guess without reading the magazine: sagging interest.

—Elliott Harris of the *Chicago Sun-Times*, on baseball's buxom Morganna the Kissing Bandit telling *Sports Illustrated* why she decided to retire

And so they escorted her off the field, two a breast.

—Sportswriter Si Burick, on the removal of Morganna the Kissing Bandit from a major league baseball game

They shouldn't throw at me. I'm the father of five or six kids.

—Ex-major-leaguer Tito Fuentes, after getting hit by a pitch

FREUDIAN QUIPS

I was trying to hit my in-laws.

—Atlanta Braves pitcher Greg Maddux, on throwing a ball into the stands to celebrate his career-high fourteen strikeouts in a 1–0 win over Milwaukee

After his Tigers beat the Blue Jays the other day, manager Alan Trammell said, "[Winning] never gets old." Heck, at the rate the Tigers are going, it may never get to puberty.

—Steve Ziants of the *Pittsburgh Post-Gazette*

According to the *Sporting News*, over the last four years, Wade Boggs hit .800 with women in scoring position.

—David Letterman, on the ongoing Wade Boggs–Margo Adams revelations

Everybody got married in the off-season. We might have the best road record in baseball this season.

—Newlywed Boston Red Sox reliever Wes Gardner

That's like Miss Piggy claiming the only difference between her and Bo Derek is her body.

—Jim Reeves, *Fort Worth Star-Telegram* sportswriter, on the claim by Montreal Expos' pitcher Floyd Youmans that the only difference between him and his old buddy Dwight Gooden is his curveball

My wife wants Olympic sex—once every four years.

—Comedian Rodney Dangerfield

On CBS, they're dropping guys off on a deserted island to test their survival skills. For a real test, they should try Tonya Harding's garage.

—Mike Littwin of the *Rocky Mountain News*

Max ought to be in the Hall of Fame himself. He's fifty-six years old, and his wife's pregnant.

—Paul Hornung, ribbing teammate Max McGee during Hornung's induction into the Pro Football Hall of Fame

It was by far the greatest feeling I've ever had with my clothes on.

—Former Kansas City Royals standout George Brett, recalling the 1985 World Series Championship

It's the most exciting day I've ever had with my clothes on.

—Actress Jane Fonda in *USA Today Baseball Weekly*, after the Atlanta Braves won the World Series

DETROIT SHOCK FORWARD ASTOU NDIAYE-DIATTA GAVE BIRTH TO TRIPLETS IN APRIL, ONE YEAR AFTER THE CLEVELAND ROCKERS' HELEN DARLING DID THE SAME. ALERT STATISTICIANS IMMEDIATELY CREDITED THE WNBA WITH PRO BASKETBALL'S FIRST TRIPLET-DOUBLE.

—Dwight Perry of the *Seattle Times*

Float like a butterfly, sting like a B-cup?

—Headline in the *San Diego Union-Tribune*, after Christy Martin grabbed Laila Ali's bra when the news conference for their fight turned into a scuffle

On the bright side, look at this—the guy spent seventy-two hours in a Marine Corps barracks, tying the old record held by Madonna.

—David Letterman, on boxer Riddick Bowe

As long as Boris Spassky and Bobby Fischer keep their shirts on, I have no problem with it.

—Gavin McDougald of couchmaster.ca, after chess grandmaster Maria Manakova posed nude in Russian men's magazines

The Los Angeles Dodgers turned their first triple play in over forty-seven years. That is, of course, if you don't include the time Steve Garvey got two women pregnant while he was engaged to a third.

—Comedy writer Jerry Perisho

Cindy Crawford said she's looking for a man to have a baby with her. And you thought the lines were long for Yankee tickets.

—Conan O'Brien of NBC

This'll be the most interesting honeymoon in history. They've asked the hotel for a spotter.

—Comedian Argus Hamilton, on former Olympic gold medalist Nadia Comaneci returning home to Romania to marry U.S. champion gymnast Bart Conner

I guess in this case, the sword was mightier than the pen.

—Ex-Olympic gymnast Bart Conner, on Romanian soldiers who protected Comaneci from the media during their wedding in Bucharest

Andy, baby, those are the cheerleaders.

—Wanda Sykes on HBO's *Inside the NFL*, after Andy Rooney said female sideline reporters don't know what they're talking about

According to a new survey, 76 percent of men would rather watch football games than have sex . . . See, the other 24 percent live in areas where all they get on TV are New York Jets games.

—Jay Leno

Kurt would first like to thank his wife for everything he's ever done.

—Brenda Warner, wife of St. Louis Rams quarterback Kurt Warner, speaking at a news conference to announce Warner's MVP award, because he had been told to rest his ailing vocal cords

Mike Ditka has been chosen as spokesman for Levitra, a new impotency drug. The manufacturer originally wanted to sign a placekicker, to go along with the slogan: "It's up, and it's good!"

—Comedian and broadcaster Jim Barach

Michael is just getting too old for the game. In fact, Nike just introduced its latest line of shoes, the I Need Some Air Jordans.

—Jim Barach, on Michael Jordan nearing the end of his NBA career

I was expecting to find blood. Instead we saw this beautiful blond in the front row. That's why we stayed out there so long.

—Phil Jackson, Chicago Bulls coach, explaining why he loitered under the basket after it was determined Michael Jordan had not been seriously injured during a spill

I want to be the fastest woman in the world . . . in a manner of speaking.

—Race car driver Shirley Muldowney

We get up close and a little too personal.

—Don Taylor of Sportsnet (Canada), previewing a piece on Paul Tracy in which the driver reveals he does not use underwear

No clue as to how the services will be staged, but the possibilities for the wedding vows are mind-boggling. To have and to clutch? Till death do us pit? I now pronounce you mechanic and wife?

—Dwight Perry of the *Seattle Times*, after Darlington Raceway sold out all its available wedding packages in which race-goers will get hitched at the South Carolina track before NASCAR's Southern 500

One rumor: When Viagra mechanics popped the hood, they couldn't get it back down.

—Martin Fennelly of the *Tampa Tribune*, after the Viagra car failed to make the field for the Daytona 500

I don't want to catch anything. That thing has been passed around more often than Paris Hilton.

—Boston Red Sox GM Theo Epstein to ESPN.com, on why he avoids the World Series trophy

CHAPTER 4

BAD BOYS, BAD BOYS! (BAD GIRLS, BAD GIRLS?)

Everybody loves Mike Tyson, Tonya Harding, and Dennis Rodman. Or, more precisely, everybody loves to laugh or shake their heads at the most outrageous people in sports. From run-ins with the law to simple stupidity, the sports world is no different than the rest of society. Tyson, Harding, and Rodman are certainly not alone—notoriety is alive and well among the athletes we love to loathe.

Reaction was swift. Afterward President Bush telephoned him in the locker room and offered to name him ambassador to France.

—Comedian Argus Hamilton, after Randy Moss pretended to moon the Green Bay crowd following a touchdown celebration in a 2005 playoff game

Randy spent a night in jail. He used his one phone call to tell Daunte Culpepper that he was open.

—Bill Scheft of *Sports Illustrated*, on the arrest of former Vikings receiver Randy Moss

Based on Moss' off-the-field episodes, he's probably also the best player hands up.

—Joe Knowles of the *Chicago Tribune*, after Marshall coach Bob Pruett said that his top wide receiver, Randy Moss, was "hands down, the best player in college football"

The WWF offers . . . Tyson bites.

—Headline in *USA Today*

We took two different paths in life. I scramble people's brains, and he fixes 'em.

—Heavyweight Mike Tyson, on the fact that his brother Rodney is a surgical assistant

What tribe? The knucklehead tribe?

—TNT commentator Charles Barkley, after being told Mike Tyson's new facial tattoo was a tribal thing

[He] called me a "rapist" and a "recluse." I'm not a recluse.

—Mike Tyson, on writer Wallace Matthews

You can't put this on family television. It would be more like a sick-com.

—Mike Tyson, on his domestic life in Las Vegas with his thirteen-year-old daughter, his sixteen-year-old niece, and his nine-month-old baby

Mike Tyson was a referee at Wrestlemania 14, and at the end of the night he gave the crowd the finger. The weird part is it was Evander Holyfield's finger.

—NBC's Conan O'Brien

It's been reported that Mike Tyson slapped Don King and kicked him in the face several times. A spokesman for the Nevada Boxing Commission said, "This is the exact kind of behavior that could get Tyson reinstated in boxing."

—Conan O'Brien

I'd like to suggest a working title. *Ear Factor*.

—Broadcaster Keith Olbermann, on a proposed reality show where contestants would fight Tyson

A TV producer is now putting together a new reality show in which an average guy will train for six months and then step into the boxing ring with Mike Tyson. I think the name of the show is *Joe Moron*.

—*Tonight Show* host Jay Leno

If Mike Tyson took that kind of vow of abstinence, he'd probably knock the other guy out during the weigh-in.

—Jim Hodges of the *Newport News Daily Press*, on Lennox Lewis going six weeks without sex as part of his training for his heavyweight title fight against Vitali Klitschko

It's good that Mike Tyson has been granted parole. More steps like this must be taken to make our prisons safer places.

—Greg Cote of the *Miami Herald*

He's already on probation for four years. One more arrest, and he'll be eligible to play football for Nebraska.

—Comedian Argus Hamilton, on Mike Tyson

Boxing is full of thieves, crooks, and liars . . . and those are the good guys.

—Tim Leiweke, president of the Anschutz Entertainment Group, in the *Los Angeles Times*

Hockey card collectors take note: There are rumors next year's card may feature both a front and side view.

—Vancouver Global TV sportscaster Squire Barnes, on the assault conviction handed Vancouver Canucks forward Donald Brashear

Maybe it should have been a clue that he kept his mask on when he left the rink.

—Tom FitzGerald of the *San Francisco Chronicle*, on Hungarian hockey goalie Attila Ambrus being jailed for seventeen years after police discovered what his day job was: robbing banks—twenty-nine of them in total

Bruins star Joe Thornton was charged with assault after getting into a bar fight while celebrating his older brother's graduation from law school. Tight family, those Thorntons, making sure the graduate got an immediate client base.

—Steve Rosenbloom of the *Chicago Tribune*

Danton's supporters are hoping the agent gets 10 percent of that.

—Michael Ventre of msnbc.com, on Mike Danton of the St. Louis Blues facing a possible seven-year prison sentence for plotting to have his agent killed

He's been very talkative, but usually it's under oath.

—Oakland Athletics general manager Sandy Alderson, on Albert Belle of the White Sox and his attempt to spruce up his image

Do you know what that means? His control is back.

—Bill Scheft of *Sports Illustrated*, on Phillies closer José Mesa, who said if he faced former Indians teammate Omar Vizquel ten times, he would hit him ten times

If he ever decides to write a book, I've already got the title: *The Bases Were Loaded and So Was I.*

—*San Francisco Examiner* columnist Art Spander, on reliever Steve Howe, arrested for drugs seven times

I dunno. I never smoked any Astroturf.

—Former New York Mets pitcher Tug McGraw, asked whether he preferred grass or Astroturf

Darryl Strawberry will be paid $500,000 for the rest of the season, plus he gets to keep whatever he finds in Steve Howe's locker.

—David Letterman of CBS

I see they put us together: assault and battery.

—Darryl Strawberry, noticing that his locker was next to that of another player who had off-season legal troubles, pitcher Dwight Gooden

Do you think they'll change Yankee Stadium's nickname to "The Halfway House That Ruth Built"?

—Bob Lacey of the *Half Moon Bay (CA) Review*, after hearing the Yankees are interested in signing Darryl Strawberry and Dwight Gooden

In Dover, New Hampshire, the city's famed drug-detecting police dog has retired after sniffing out over $200,000 worth of illegal drugs. That beats Darryl Strawberry's old record.

—Jay Leno

DESPITE HIS AGE, THE TEAM FIGURES HE'S STILL GOT SOME GREAT STUFF. AND HE KEEPS IT IN A POUCH IN HIS LOCKER.

—Comedy writer Alan Ray, on the Yankees signing pitcher Dwight Gooden

The Mets are helping out with drug testing. Martha Stewart is going to make Olympic license plates for the next three to five years, unless she plea bargains. And Winona Ryder is getting us all the Olympic uniforms for free.

—Comedian Billy Crystal, on why New York would be the perfect city to host the 2012 Summer Olympics

Art Howe plans to clamp down with new curfew rules during spring training such as everyone in their rooms by 11 P.M. and grow-lights out at twelve.

—Dwight Perry of the *Seattle Times*, on the marijuana-loving New York Mets and their new manager

Might explain why the team lost fifteen straight games at home. Tough to get upset about losing at home when you don't even know you're home.

—T. J. Simers of the *Los Angeles Times*, on allegations that eleven New York Mets were using marijuana

I'm a traditionalist, but I think it's a nice touch that the Mets, for their seventh-inning stretch song, have replaced "Take Me Out to the Ball Game" with "Puff the Magic Dragon."

—Scott Ostler of the *San Francisco Chronicle*, on the New York Mets and their marijuana problems

This SARS scare has people in the athletic world spooked about dealing with the public. I hear Mike Price won't give autographs to his lap dancers.

—Scott Ostler, after Alabama fired football coach Mike Price following an evening at a topless bar

I finally admit the University of Oklahoma has outdone Oklahoma State University this year by a 3–0–1 score. The Cowboys tied the Sooners in cheating, but got beat in alleged rapes, shootings, and drug deals.

—Dave Brenner, in a letter to the *Daily Oklahoman* on the Sooners' football troubles

Warren Sapp, who allegedly tested positive for marijuana several times at the University of Miami, was in an awful hurry to sign with Tampa Bay after he found out the Bucs play on grass.

—Mark Kriegel of the *New York Daily News*

Hurricane season has started in southern Florida. In fact, winds were so strong they actually knocked a player on the University of Miami football team into a classroom.

—Jay Leno

The school is offering a $2,500 reward and a full scholarship to Miami.

—Bill Scheft of *Sports Illustrated*, on Florida State's two stolen national championship football trophies

Athletic Director Skip Bertman says he wants to stop drunks from attending LSU's home football games. Well, there goes the program.

—Jerry Greene in the *Orlando Sentinel*

Some question his ability to really understand pro football. After all, he's never spent one day in jail.

—Comedy writer Alan Ray, on the hiring of comedian Dennis Miller by *Monday Night Football*

It's great that Andre still carries the torch for her.

—Cary Sekoff in the *San Francisco Chronicle*, after Raiders receiver Andre "Bad Moon" Rison announced that he will marry longtime girlfriend and rap star Lisa "Left Eye" Lopes, who burned down his $1 million Atlanta home

Does this mean his victory in that bar fight a while back will be declared a no contest?

—Dan Daly of the *Washington Times*, on José Canseco testing positive for steroids

The Hall of Fame has announced that if José Canseco is inducted, he'll go in wearing an orange jumpsuit and his jersey number—16843.

—Jim Armstrong of the *Denver Post*

Hey, Nate, I hear the Dallas Cowboys are going to retire your number: 85J9302.

—Former major-leaguer John Kruk, commenting on Nate Newton getting pulled over for felony marijuana possession

Do you know what they are calling a police lineup in Dallas? A huddle.

—John McClain of the *Houston Chronicle*

He always lines up near the hash marks.

—Comedy writer Alan Ray, on Dallas Cowboys wide receiver Michael Irvin facing drug charges

Here now are the NFL matchups for next weekend: You have the Patriots vs. the Jaguars, you have the Packers vs. the Panthers, you have the People vs. the Dallas Cowboys.

—David Letterman

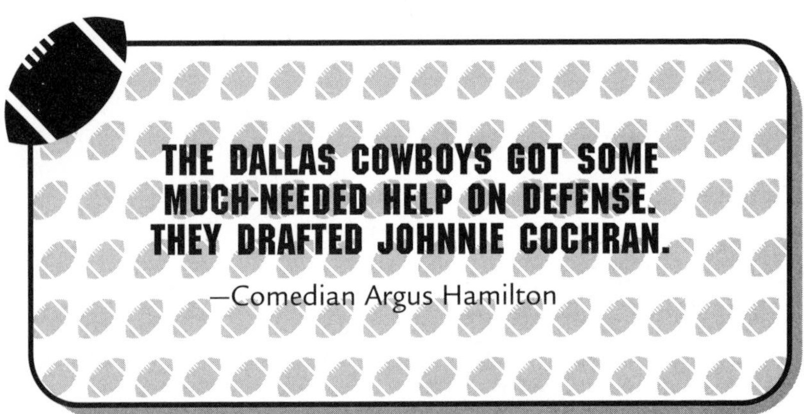

THE DALLAS COWBOYS GOT SOME MUCH-NEEDED HELP ON DEFENSE. THEY DRAFTED JOHNNIE COCHRAN.

—Comedian Argus Hamilton

The Cowboys are interested in that idea, too. They are working with the courts on how to charge admission for their parole hearings.

—Janice Hough in the *San Francisco Chronicle*, on the Washington Redskins' plan to charge admission for practice sessions

I saw something nice today. This was a good little gesture. Two members of the Dallas Cowboys were actually standing in front of a police station autographing mug shots for the kids.

—Jay Leno

What do you call the University of Arizona football player caught with eighty-seven pounds of marijuana? A Dallas Cowboys first-rounder.

—Steve Hummer in the *Atlanta Journal-Constitution*

To me, it won't really be a Cowboys car unless Michael Irvin is handcuffed in the back seat.

—Bill Scheft of *Sports Illustrated*, on the Dallas Cowboys' plans to sponsor a Winston Cup car

There can be no debate as to this year's NFL MVP: That's Ray Lewis' defense attorney, Ed Garland.

—Mark Kriegel of the *New York Daily News*

Several organizations will be looking for the next Ray Lewis . . . the Bucs, the 49ers, the Police . . .

—Comedy writer Alan Ray, on the NFL draft

That's perfect: Prime Time joins Crime Time.

—Ian Hamilton of the *Regina Leader-Post*, after Deion Sanders signed with the Baltimore Ravens, making him a teammate of tailback Jamal Lewis, arrested on drug-related charges, and linebacker Ray Lewis, who once was charged with murder

Dennis McKinley, the Arizona Cardinals' backup fullback, allegedly had an AR-15 rifle among eleven guns when police arrested him as part of a marijuana-trafficking operation. McKinley's lawyers are expected to pin the blame on the Cardinals, who had challenged him to become more of a weapon next season.

—Dwight Perry of the *Seattle Times*

To give you an idea how bad the team is doing, he tried to run for it and lost three yards.

—Jay Leno, on Arizona Cardinals fullback Dennis McKinley's drug-dealing arrest

Are you familiar with arena football? That's where the players commit crimes indoors.

—Jay Leno, on the arrest of former NFL quarterback Todd Marinovich, attempting a comeback in arena football

Age is a factor. He can no longer outrun those bigger, stronger, and younger police officers.

—Comedy writer Alan Ray, on running back Lawrence Phillips leaving the Canadian Football League's Montreal Alouettes for the second time

Maybe they should give him O. J.'s.

—Bob Lacey of the *Half Moon Bay (CA) Review*, after Nebraska tailback Lawrence Phillips said he made a mistake when he attacked his former girlfriend, and he still wants a shot at the Heisman Trophy

Cornhusker football players can graduate after two terms—one for assault and one for armed robbery.

—Comedian Argus Hamilton, after several members of the Nebraska football team were charged with various crimes, including one for attempted murder

They're rioting in Oakland. So this is supposed to be news? Meanwhile, it's chaos in Tampa. Six retirement homes reported residents turning over checkerboards and throwing Jell-O.

—Jeff Schultz in the *Atlanta Journal-Constitution*, after the Buccaneers won the Super Bowl

That looks like the Mr. T starter set.

—Glen Suitor of The Sports Network (Toronto), on the several pounds of jewelry worn by injured Toronto Argos receiver Derrell Mitchell during a sideline interview

Osama bin Laden, Bar-b-que at your house . . . We will deliver.

—Banner put up by baseball fans in St. Louis at Busch Stadium following the 9/11 terrorist attacks

Let me see if I've got this straight: Pete Rose may have violated the terms of his lifetime ban. The baseball commissioner's office says they'll investigate the incident, then take "appropriate action." Does this mean Rose's lifetime ban might be extended?

—Bob Lacey, *Half Moon Bay (CA) Review*

Was David Wells begging to join the party, and, second, was Sammy Sosa there to clean up the corks?

—Karl Vogel of the *Lincoln (NE) Journal Star*, after the New York Yankees delivered a postgame bottle of champagne to each of the six Houston Astros pitchers who combined to no-hit them

If the cork fits, they can't acquit.

—Mike Downey, of the *Chicago Tribune*, on Sammy Sosa using a corked bat

If the signal does not transmit, you must acquit!

—Greg Cote of the *Miami Herald*, on Johnnie Cochran's defense if the O. J. Simpson satellite-TV piracy case goes to trial

How much do you want to bet that Simpson backs out for the most obvious reason: He can't find a pair of gloves that fit?

—Randy Turner of the *Winnipeg Free Press*, about a celebrity boxing match featuring Joey Buttafuoco and O. J. Simpson

If O. J. Simpson were a Canuck, Burke would defend him too.

—Nick Kypreos of Sportsnet TV (Canada), on Canucks general manager Brian Burke defending Donald Brashear and other Vancouver players

There's about as much of a chance of getting a straight answer from a general manager as O. J. Simpson has of making the jury in the Jayson Williams trial.

—R. J. Broadhead of Sportsnet TV (Canada), before the NHL trading deadline

The school has hired Johnnie Cochran to try and prove that Simpson was never there.

—Michael Ventre of msnbc.com, on O. J. Simpson visiting USC's football practice

O. J. Simpson attends the [2005] Orange Bowl. And that was nice: He left two tickets at will-call under "killers, real."

—Bill Scheft of *Sports Illustrated*

It was unanimous, one to nothing.

—NBA commissioner David Stern, explaining how he suspended Indiana Pacers' forward Ron Artest for the rest of the season after he went into the stands after a fan in Detroit

Alert NBA statisticians immediately credited Forte with the off-season's first triple-trouble.

—Dwight Perry of the *Seattle Times*, on Sonics guard Joe Forte being charged with speeding, drug possession, and illegal gun possession all in one day

It turns out that Iverson doesn't lead the 76ers in steals after all.

—Dwight Perry, after John Croce, the brother of Philadelphia 76ers owner Pat Croce, was fired as the team's conditioning coach after videotape evidence showed him removing money from Allen Iverson's pants

As I understand it, the ruckus started when they tried to stuff 68.5 cents into a G-string.

—Bill Scheft of *Sports Illustrated*, after three Milwaukee Bucks were arrested for an incident outside a Toronto strip club

Sounds like Webber was the leader of the Fib Five.

—Steve Rosenbloom of the *Chicago Tribune*, on Chris Webber of the Sacramento Kings, who was being indicted for lying to a grand jury about being paid while at Michigan, where he led the so-called Fab Five

Patrick Ewing will have his number retired by the New York Knicks on February 28. The tribute will come three years to the day after his pants were retired in a touching ceremony at Atlanta's Gold Club.

—Scott Feschuk of the *National (Toronto) Post*

They're falling faster than Patrick Ewing's pants at the Gold Club.

—David Amber of The Sports Network (Canada), on the pace of baseball records

This was the largest organized group of nudes since the New York Knicks visited the Gold Club in Atlanta.

—Comedian Jerry Perisho, on hearing that more than 2,000 people posed nude in downtown Montreal for a photo shoot

Patrick Ewing retires, and the honors pour in. At Atlanta's Gold Club, they've announced that no other patron will ever wear Ewing's lap dancer.

—Scott Ostler of the *San Francisco Chronicle*

That was a real eye-opener for me, walking down the corridors in prison and having people walk up and say, "Hey, Caminiti, sign my crack pipe."

—Former National League MVP Ken Caminiti, who died of a heart attack at age forty-one, on serving jail time for a drug conviction

No, he likes to smoke his pipe full.

—An unidentified snowboard enthusiast, responding to a question if Canadian snowboard Olympic gold medalist Ross Rebagliati, whose result was called into question because he tested positive for marijuana, would compete in the halfpipe snowboard event

I love the Olympic motto—"Swifter, Higher, Stronger." Who in Canada was stronger than 1950s weightlifter Doug Hepburn? Who was swifter than Ben Johnson, Donovan Bailey, or Harry Jerome? And who was higher than Ross Rebagliati?

—Cam Hutchinson of the *Saskatoon StarPhoenix*

Prediction: By the time the Winter Olympics get to Vancouver in 2010, marijuana will be legal in Canada. Prediction, Part II: Our snowboarding team will be smokin', dude!

—Randy Turner of the *Winnipeg Free Press*

I think my favorite sport in the Olympics is the one in which you make your way through the snow, you stop, you shoot a gun, and then you continue on. In most of the world, it is known as the biathlon, except in New York City, where it is known as winter.

—Michael Ventre of msnbc.com

Legal pit stops.

—Headline in the *Budapest Sun*, after the Formula One Hungarian Grand Grix canceled a one-year experiment with legalized prostitution at the racetrack

The Casey Martin decision was expected . . . This Supreme Court has already shown themselves sympathetic to those unable to compete without their help, witness the presidential election.

—Janice Hough in the *San Francisco Chronicle*

DENNIS RODMAN PLAYS A VILLAIN IN THE MOVIE *DOUBLE TEAM*. THAT'S LIKE HIRING ELIZABETH TAYLOR TO PLAY A DIVORCEE.

—Tom Powers of the *St. Paul Pioneer-Press*

How do you say Merry Christmas to a Portland Trail Blazer? "Police Navidad."

—Dwight Perry of the *Seattle Times*, on the law-breaking NBA team in Portland

Political wags are warning that Canada's proposal to legalize small amounts of marijuana could strain relations with the United States. That's certainly not true in the NBA, where Portland players have volunteered to relocate north of the border as the Trail, B.C., Blazers.

—Dwight Perry

After vowing to create a new image after fifteen player arrests and twenty suspensions during the reign of president Bob Whitsitt, the Portland Trail Blazers tipped off the post-Whitsitt era by drafting a guy named Travis Outlaw.

—Dwight Perry

Amazing. Twenty-nine teams in the NBA, and the "Jail Blazers" are the ones who draft Travis Outlaw.

—Jim Armstrong of the *Denver Post*

When he comes through the door, they now strike up the band and play "Inhale to the Chief."

—Kevin McHale of the Boston Celtics, ribbing former Celtics teammate Robert Parrish for his arrest on marijuana charges

As long as his joints hold up.

—Columnist Peter Vescey, on how long veteran Robert Parrish might keep playing in the NBA

If NBA commissioner David Stern is really committed to bringing fans closer to the action, why not invite them to arraignments?

—Peter Vecsey

Marijuana testing is coming to the NBA? OK. So where are they going to find all the replacement players?

—Greg Cote of the *Miami Herald*

Canadian Interuniversity Sport, the NCAA north, has decreed that athletes won't get scholarships, starting in 2004, unless they attain a 65 percent average. Some misguided basketball players, we hear, misunderstood the ruling and immediately signed up for foul-shooting lessons.

—Dwight Perry of the *Seattle Times*

Yeah, we were on the first floor.

—Former NBA star Charles Barkley, when asked by a judge if he had any regrets for throwing a five-foot-two guy through a barroom window

Maybe I need to write a book and say I was misquoted, or punch somebody in Milwaukee.

—Michael Jordan of the Chicago Bulls, after being informed that he trailed Charles Barkley in NBA all-star voting

At first, I thought it was a defamation of character. Then I realized, I have no character.

—Charles Barkley, after Tonya Harding referred to herself as the Charles Barkley of figure skating

Sure I do. After all, I know Tonya Harding.

—PGA golfer Peter Jacobsen, after a fan in the gallery said he still had a chance to win a tournament even though he was several strokes off the pace

Somewhere out there, Tonya Harding must feel the urge to crash her truck into the side of an outhouse.

—Jeff Gordon of the *St. Louis Post-Dispatch*, after José Canseco got busted for steroids and Mike Tyson got arrested for a street brawl in roughly twenty-four hours

Tonya's weapon was a hubcap or, as the police report called it, "her best dinnerware."

—Comedy writer Jerry Perisho, after Harding bloodied her boyfriend's face in a fight after a round of video poker

When asked why she attacked her boyfriend, she said: "I would have hired somebody to do it, but good help is so hard to find these days."

—Comedian Alex Kaseberg, after Tonya Harding pleaded not guilty to charges she threw a hubcap at her boyfriend and bloodied his face by punching him

Major League Baseball is enlarging the strike zone to include the kneecap: It's called the Tonya Harding rule.

—Alex Kaseberg

It's irreconcilable differences. He sits around the house every night, while everybody knows how she likes to go out clubbing.

—Argus Hamilton, on Tonya Harding filing for divorce

AFTER SEEING TONYA HARDING DRESSED AS MRS. CLAUS, IT CERTAINLY IS EASIER TO UNDERSTAND WHY SANTA STAYS OUT ALL NIGHT.

—Gary Shelton of the *St. Petersburg Times*, on Harding's Christmas skating exhibition in Portland

He turned in a typical performance. He slurred the first nine men he faced.

—Comedy writer Alan Ray, after Atlanta Braves pitcher John Rocker worked his first game in spring training

Looks like that sensitivity training is really paying dividends. Instead of insulting gays, minorities, and immigrants, Rocker insulted reporters, English teachers, and the hearing impaired.

—Columnist Scott Ostler, after Atlanta Braves closer John Rocker told reporters after his first game back from his suspension, "I ain't sayin' nothin' to nobody. Are you deaf? Beat it, media."

John Rocker, in an attempt to show what a nice guy he really is, is buying 100 tickets a game for underprivileged rednecks in the Atlanta area.

—Jim Armstrong of the *Denver Post*

Wouldn't that be sweet justice, for Rocker to be sent to a place where he's a foreigner?

—Randy Harvey of the *Los Angeles Times*, on a report that the Atlanta Braves might trade John Rocker to Montreal for Ugueth Urbina

Her players must have been grateful to survive the final cuts.

—Columnist Chris Inglis, after a woman who was coaching a junior high volleyball team in Rockford, Illinois, was arrested and later fired because she got a meat cleaver from her car and tried to take it into the school after exchanging heated words with a female spectator

Olympic skating champion Oksana Baiul was charged with drunk driving in Connecticut. They took her blood alcohol level, and she received .18, .16, .17, .16, .16, and .17.

—Comic Don McMillan

If it turns out that Barry Bonds used steroids to bulk up and add muscle mass, he could get four to eight years as governor of California.

—Comedian Argus Hamilton

CHAPTER 5

TIPPING THE SCALES

The real Battle of the Bulge was decided conclusively, but lives on in spirit in the sporting world. From Refrigerator Perry's famous fight with his waistline, to the lack of muscle on Manute Bol's seven-foot-seven frame, the scales can tell the tale. The sports version of the Battle of the Bulge will live on, seemingly forever because in sports, size does matter.

Not that Reid needs to lose a few pounds, but it took three containers of Gatorade to douse him after the [2005] NFC Championship Game.

—Jim Armstrong, of aol.com, on the size of Philadelphia Eagles coach Andy Reid

It's gut-wrenching, and I have a lot of gut to wrench.

—Eagles coach Andy Reid, after Philadelphia blew a ten-point lead in the final eight minutes of a game against Arizona

Pork Chop's major at Mississippi State was fitness management.

—Jeff Gordon of the *St. Louis Post-Dispatch*, after the Seattle Seahawks drafted 345-pound guard Pork Chop Womack

It doesn't fit right for me, doesn't look right. I need some more curves.

—Oakland Raiders 325-pound tackle Robert Gallery, on why he changed his jersey number from seventy-four to seventy-six

But Akebono wants it made clear that he wears the diaper in the family.

—Steve Rosenbloom of the *Chicago Tribune*, after the wife of Akebono, the Hawaiian-born sumo grandmaster, gave birth to a seven-pound, seven-ounce daughter

It's getting out of hand in the PGA. First, Casey Martin sues so he can use a golf cart. Now Craig Stadler is suing the PGA so he can use a dessert cart.

—Brian McKenna of KFNS-AM in St. Louis

We look like the number ten.

—New York City Technical College basketball coach Mike Eisenberg, who is five foot ten and 220 pounds, describing what happens when he stands next to his guard Martin Lacewell, who is six foot six and 133 pounds

You know what we're going to have with all those weight clauses? Twenty-five Manute Bols.

—Chicago Cubs pitcher Rick Sutcliffe, on spring training weight requirements

Actually, Manute was only the second choice for the publicity stunt. The Indianapolis Ice originally tried to talk John Henry Williams into letting them use Ted Williams.

—Dan Daly of the *Washington Times*, on Manute Bol's brief stint with Indianapolis of the Central Hockey League

The NBA has never seen anything so big and so quick that didn't have advertising on its side.

—Thomas Bonk of the *Los Angeles Times*, on Charles Barkley

He was so fat, he fell down and rocked himself to sleep trying to get up.

—Pat Williams, recalling his days as general manager of the Philadelphia 76ers, on the first time he tried to put Charles Barkley on the scales

Charles joined my family for a day at the beach and my children asked if they could go in the ocean. I had to tell them, "Not right now, kids. Charles is using it."

—Pat Williams, on 260-pound rookie power forward Charles Barkley

I can't use those fat jokes anymore. Stanley has turned over a new chin.

—Pat Williams, on NBA player Stanley Roberts when his weight dropped under 300 pounds

McDonald's and Wendy's are suing Stanley for nonsupport.

—Pat Williams, on a new slimmer Stanley Roberts

He could be the poster boy for jelly doughnuts. When he was here, we had to remove an obstruction from his throat. It was a pizza.

—Pat Williams, picking on Stanley Roberts

It was a weekend of brilliant and short people. I was brilliant, the rest of them were short.

—Former Celtics star Larry Bird, recalling his all-star experience in Dallas

The boss was pretty happy. He found somebody who could wash roofs on vans.

—Zdeno Chara, the six-foot-nine Ottawa Senators defenseman from Slovakia, on working in a car wash during the offseason in Prince George, British Columbia, home to his former junior team, the Cougars

The most intense Hitchcock gets is eating Ho Ho's from his armchair. I don't need respect from some guy who has watched the game his whole life from the couch.

—Tampa Bay Lightning defenseman Bryan Marchment, on Dallas Stars coach Ken Hitchcock, after Hitchcock called Marchment a liability on the ice

He put a neutral-zone trap in front of his refrigerator.

—Bill Scheft of *Sports Illustrated*, on how Toronto Maple Leafs Coach Pat Quinn lost fifty-five pounds in the summer of 2002

He said he was going to put on twenty-five pounds of muscle. Instead, it looks like twenty-five pounds of Molsons.

—Then-Los Angeles Kings coach Pat Quinn, commenting on forward Danny Gratton's appearance at training camp

As they already had center Doug Weight in their lineup, the Oilers now have both Hajt and Weight.

—Garth Woolsey of the *Toronto Star*, after the Edmonton Oilers recalled defenseman Chris Hajt (pronounced "Hite") from their farm team

Deion is truly one of a kind . . . He plays two pro sports and doesn't hit in either one of them.

—Comedian Jerry Perisho, on outfielder Deion Sanders, also an NFL cornerback, barely hitting his weight

At 260 pounds, quarterback Ryan Leaf is not taking his second chance lightly.

—Bud Geracie of the *San Jose Mercury News*

How far Drew Bledsoe can take Buffalo this season remains to be seen, but with an offensive line that averages six foot four and 331 pounds, you have to admit that the 2003 Bills, at the very least, look like a team of density.

—Dwight Perry of the *Seattle Times*

Keith Traylor said he went to a nutritionist to get in better shape for the upcoming season. Seems to me a couple of laps around Ted Washington would have done it.

—Steve Rosenbloom of the *Chicago Tribune*, talking about two massive Chicago Bears tackles

That's like saying Ally McBeal was jammed into Tony Siragusa's pants.

—Columnist Gary Means, after XFL commentator Jim Ross exclaimed: "Over 30,000 fans have jammed the L.A. Coliseum." The place holds 90,000

Tony was told one must have a healthy body and sound mind . . . He thought he had to make a choice.

—Tony Kornheiser of the *Washington Post*, on Baltimore Ravens defensive tackle Tony Siragusa

He weighs 320. He's got a lot of backside.

—Tony Kornheiser, of ESPN's *Pardon the Interruption*, after New Orleans Saints coach Jim Haslett said the reason for drafting Johnathan Sullivan was that "He's got a lot of upside"

THE WAY HE LOOKS, THERE SHOULD BE A MCDONALD'S NEXT TO HIS HOUSE.

—New York Giants sackmaster Michael Strahan, taking a shot at all-pro defensive tackle Warren Sapp

Square isn't the shape I'd associate with Warren.

—Michael Lough of the *Macon (GA) Telegraph*, on the Oakland Raiders' 300-pound Warren Sapp appearing on TV's *Hollywood Squares*

Getting up in the middle of the night for feedings at 1 A.M., 3 A.M., and five o'clock in the morning . . . kind of like I do for myself.

—Six-foot-four, 275-pound University of Kentucky football player Jared Lorenzen, on being a new father

I wasn't that worried about him until I read in their press guide that he was born on November 1, 15, and 16.

—Citadel football coach Art Baker, on six-foot-six, 310-pound Vanderbilt offensive tackle Ronald Hale

When he runs the ball we use a lot more film.

—Minnesota Vikings coach Dennis Green, on slow-footed quarterback Sean Salisbury

I see that Tony Gwynn signed a contract with an incentive clause based on plate appearances . . . from the looks of Tony, he must've thought they meant dinner plates.

—Columnist Jerry Klein

The Yanks look like Rosie O'Donnell trying to hold off Michael Phelps in the 100 butterfly.

—Joel Sherman of the *New York Post*, after the New York Yankees had a ten-and-a-half game lead over the Boston Red Sox quickly reduced to three and a half in the American League East pennant race

Let's not overdo this. I only have to call the bases, I don't have to steal them.

—Baseball umpire Eric Gregg, to a trainer helping him lose some of his 300-plus pounds

He makes a great hitting background.

—Philadelphia Phillies broadcaster Rich Ashburn, on 300-pound John McSherry umpiring at second base

If he raced his pregnant wife he'd finish third.

—Former Los Angeles Dodgers manager Tommy Lasorda, on his catcher, Mike Scioscia

If Vaughn weighed in at 275 pounds last season, so did Rhode Island.

—Mike Lupica of the *New York Daily News*, on Mo Vaughn and his listed weight in the New York Mets media guide

The Reds media guide lists him at 210. We have seen him now, finally, in the considerable flesh, and we can say this: That 210, it's from the chin up.

—*Cincinnati Post* columnist Paul Daugherty, on Cincinnati Reds outfielder Kevin Mitchell

Like putting just one more suitcase on the *Queen Mary*.

—Pittsburgh Pirates trainer Kent Biggerstaff, after hearing that 240-pound pitcher Rick Reuschel had a four-pound weight gain

He gives new meaning to that term Big Red Machine.

—Phillies pitcher Larry Andersen, with his assessment of the excess poundage of Cincinnati replacement pitcher Pedro Borbon

No truth to the rumor the specialty of the house is Special K.

—Jayson Stark of the *Philadelphia Inquirer* after Pete Incaviglia, who used to pile up the strikeouts as a free swinger in the big leagues, opened a new restaurant in Texas called Inky's Place

Toronto pitcher David Wells was so disgusted with the *Sports Illustrated* cover depicting him as a big fat slob that he ate the first 50,000 copies.

—Baseball enthusiast Terry Toll

And that figure jumps to more than $850 million once David Wells returns his empties.

—Bill Scheft of *Sports Illustrated*, after Forbes magazine pegged the Yankees' worth at $849 million

Like they say, it ain't over till the fat guy swings.

—Philadelphia Phillies catcher Darren Daulton, on teammate and stocky first baseman John Kruk

I've reserved three seats for you at my show tonight. One for you, one for your wife, and one for your stomach.

—Comedian Don Rickles, to former major-league skipper Don Zimmer

I have to jump around in the shower to get wet.

—Ex-major-league pitcher Bruce Kison, on being six foot four and 175 pounds

I KNEW WE WERE IN TROUBLE WHEN WE GOT THERE AND THEIR CHEERLEADERS WERE BIGGER THAN US.

—Matt McDonagh, a soccer player for Highland Catholic School in St. Paul, Minnesota, after his team was eliminated in the city's elementary school playoffs

Why don't they combine this show and the beach volleyball reality series and call it *Beached Volleyball*?

—Brooks Melchior of sportsbybrooks.com, on NBC's *The Biggest Loser*, where severely overweight contestants compete to drop the most pounds

Bogues gets to play on both sides of a father-son game.

—Basketball commentator Dick Vitale, on the Charlotte Hornets five-foot-three guard Muggsy Bogues

Muggsy Bogues won, but his proximity to the table was cited as an unfair advantage.

—Dave D'Alessandro of the *Newark (NJ) Star-Ledger*, after Charles Oakley of the Toronto Raptors organized a team ping-pong tournament

This will be the first time in history a referee drops the ball rather than tosses it up.

—Dan Issel, Denver Nuggets broadcaster, before a jump ball between Denver's five-foot-eleven Michael Adams and the Charlotte Hornets' five-foot-three Muggsy Bogues

They'd better utilize him fast. Boykins was listed as five feet eight in high school, five feet seven in college, now he's five feet five. If the trend continues, bobblehead dolls will be posting this guy up.

—Scott Ostler, *San Francisco Chronicle*, on the Golden State Warriors signing diminutive Earl Boykins

Lard of the rings.

—Dwight Perry of the *Seattle Times*, on a name for the proposed fight between fifty-two-year-old Larry Holmes and balloonlike novelty boxer Eric "Butterbean" Esch

I have an advantage in this fight. I have only one chin to expose.

—Heavyweight boxer Tommy Morrison, on his bout with George Foreman

He's got a nutritionist, and I've got room service.

—George Foreman, heavyweight boxer, on the difference between his eating habits and those of Evander Holyfield

I'm not fat.

—Boxer Tex Cobb, responding to a reporter who said Cobb was a fat, cocaine-snorting drunk

One looked like a Greek god. The other looked like a Greek restaurant.

—*Los Angeles Times* columnist Jim Murray, on the Evander Holyfield–George Foreman fight

What a pity that, on Washington State's football team, Jerry Block and Kyle Stiffarm play on defense, while Billy Chase is a wide receiver and offensive lineman Sam Lightbody weighs 290 pounds.

—Tom FitzGerald of the *San Francisco Chronicle*

A [Winnipeg Blue] Bombers fan in a bar leans over to the guy next to him and says, "Wanna hear a joke about [Saskatchewan Roughrider] fans?" The guy next to him replies, "Well, before you tell that joke you should know something: I'm six feet tall and 220 pounds and I'm a 'Riders fan. The guy sitting next to me is six foot two, 240 pounds and he's a 'Riders fan, and the guy sitting next to him is six foot five, 280 pounds and he's a 'Riders fan, too. Now, do you still want to tell that joke?" The Bombers fan waves his hand and says, "Nah. Not if I'm going to have to explain it three times."

—*Winnipeg Free Press*

All the shock value of Roseanne testing positive for doughnuts.

—Randy Turner of the *Winnipeg Free Press*, on where the Oakland Raiders' Bill Romanowski testing positive for steroids rates on the surprise scale

The jockeys' biggest concern: drowning.

—Greg Cote of the *Miami Herald*, after jockeys at Florida's Gulfstream Park refused to ride because of four inches of standing water

CHAPTER 6

CALL THE NURSE, OR GET A HEARSE

Injuries and the inevitable aging process are a fact of life in all sports and at all levels and can lead to some of the funniest quips and quotes. From mind-numbing concussions, to tibias snapped like pencils, to aging baseball managers, health issues bring out some of the best one-liners in sports. Add in the steroid and blood doping scandals surrounding the Olympics, baseball, and just about every other area of competition, and the result is value-added entertainment.

Because 85 percent of Sarasota's population has also had hip replacement surgery.

—Chicago White Sox third baseman Robin Ventura, on why Bo Jackson has received so many standing ovations during spring training in Sarasota, Florida

What do Bo Jackson and rap singer Vanilla Ice have in common? Artificial hip.

—Mike Downey in the *Los Angeles Times*

I like chocolate cake.

—Quarterback Troy Aikman, when asked if the Dallas Cowboys released him due to the effects of his ten concussions

Cowboys quarterback Troy Aikman retired after a career that included three Super Bowls and ten concussions. He's now headed for a career in broadcasting. Let me tell you something, if he's going to be as good as Terry Bradshaw, he's going to need a lot more concussions.

—*Tonight Show* host Jay Leno

At least they think they did.

—Greg Cote of the *Miami Herald*, on ex-Cowboys quarterbacks Roger Staubach and Troy Aikman (who combined for about twenty career concussions) teaming up to buy a NASCAR team

Doctors say one more concussion and Steve Young's brain would be as messed up as Ryan Leaf's.

—Comedian Alex Kaseberg

I don't have one bad memory from my thirteen seasons. I don't have a memory at all, for that matter.

—Al "Bubba" Baker, recalling his career with the Cleveland Browns

He hopes to be the first NHL player to deliver an artificial hip check.

—Bill Scheft of *Sports Illustrated*, on forty-two-year-old center Igor Larionov signing with the New Jersey Devils

If I drop dead tomorrow, at least I'll know I died in good health.

—Former Houston Oilers coach Bum Phillips, after passing a physical

The embarrassing part was when one of our managers was walking with me afterward. I said, "Man, does it look like I'm walking funny?" He said, "I don't know, because I'm carrying you."

—Seattle Seahawks running back Shaun Alexander, recalling the time he got hit so hard in a team scrimmage that it dented more than his helmet

When he didn't remember our anniversary, I knew he was OK.

—Lisa McCaffrey, on the concussion suffered by her husband, Denver Broncos receiver Ed McCaffrey

I'm the kind of guy who could go into a pillow factory and walk out with a headache.

—Former University of British Columbia forward Brad Kielmann, who quit hockey after suffering eight career concussions

The possibility of a shortened season jeopardizes Eric Lindros' streak of missing at least forty games due to injuries.

—David Vecsey of espn.com, on the NHL lockout and the ramifications on the concussion-prone Lindros

Yeah, concrete.

—Indy car driver Parker Johnstone, after suffering a concussion in a crash before the Homestead Grand Prix, when asked by a hospital clerk if he was allergic to anything

Sometimes I feel like a crash-test dummy.

—John Bryan, brakeman for Dale Jarrett's team, who was run over by Ward Burton and was run over again two years later at the Brickyard 400

I'm a dentist.

—Hockey fan Marvin Watson, on why he likes the game so much

It's okay, I don't bite. Even if I did, I don't have any teeth, so it wouldn't hurt.

—Battle-scarred San Jose Sharks forward Mike Ricci, speaking to a hesitant young autograph-seeker

Good thing he didn't get me in the teeth, or I'd look just like Theo.

—Veronica Fleury, wife of Calgary Flames forward Theo Fleury, after an errant shot from Flames defenseman Zarley Zalapski hit her in the head at a game

I took five stitches. The puck took six.

—Boston Bruins equipment man Peter Henderson, after being hit on the head by a stray shot

The doctor told me, if I see two pucks, to take the one on the left.

—Boston Bruins forward Charlie Simmer, upon returning to action after an eye injury

Now I know how the slow guys feel.

—Anaheim Mighty Ducks sniper Teemu Selanne, on being hampered by an ailing thigh

I'm wondering if the team doctor of the Mighty Ducks will be referred to as "the quack."

—Kevin Dupont of the *Boston Globe*

If you've only got a day to live, come see the Maple Leafs. It'll seem like forever.

—Chicago broadcaster Pat Foley

If this treatment doesn't work out, well, wherever I go it's got to be better than Philadelphia.

—Philadelphia Flyers coach Roger Neilson, after telling his boss, Bob Clarke, he must begin chemotherapy for bone marrow cancer

TO SHOW JUST HOW AMAZING TIGER WOODS REALLY IS . . . TODAY AFTER HE WAS TRIPPED, HE WAS RUSHED OFF TO THE HOSPITAL. IN THE EXAMINING ROOM, WHEN THE DOCTOR CHECKED HIS BLOOD PRESSURE, HE WAS TWELVE UNDER.

—Comedian Jerry Perisho

The birth was attended by one doctor, two nurses, and eight NHL scouts.

—Rodney Lee of sportshollywood.com, after Wayne Gretzky's wife, Janet, gave birth to a son, Tristan

You know you're getting old when all the names in your black book have MD after them.

—Golfing legend Arnold Palmer

You know you're getting old when you go back to your class reunion and they serve prune punch.

—Golfer Chi Chi Rodriguez

I've been here so long that when I got here the Dead Sea wasn't even sick.

—Wimp Sanderson, before resigning as Alabama's basketball coach, on his thirty-two-year tenure at the school

I'm going to sell them forty-eight-minute term insurance.

—Insurance salesman and former NBA player Johnny Kerr, on the health of players participating in an NBA old-timers game

While you may not be able to contain Kobe, you can definitely contaminate him.

—Scott Howard-Cooper in the *Sacramento Bee*, after Los Angeles Lakers guard Kobe Bryant was given a bad hamburger in Sacramento that resulted in food poisoning

That may be, but it is more important that he doesn't end up the rest of his life "talking" like Walton.

—Steve Hummer of the *Atlanta Journal-Constitution*, after Shaquille O'Neal said he didn't want to spend the rest of his life walking like Bill Walton following toe surgery

And in related headlines: "Sky likely blue again," "Bengals likely bad again," and "Israelis, Palestinians likely mad at each other again."

—Mike Bianchi after his newspaper, the *Orlando Sentinel*, proclaimed "Grant Hill likely out again" in big type

It would have been less if I'd been playing.

—New Jersey Nets center Todd MacCulloch, on having to get twenty tickets for people when his team played in Seattle, even though he sat out with an injury

When I heard that a broken leg could cost him $5.3 million, I thought, hey, he's got the same hospitalization plan I've got.

—Bob Hille of the *Sporting News*, on the season-ending injury to Cleveland Browns tight end Kellen Winslow Jr.

I just hope I never get kicked in the groin.

—Broncos quarterback John Elway, on the repeated diagramming in Denver newspapers of his ruptured biceps tendon

Henry Burris sprained his left knee during an NFL Europe game and will require surgery. Nevertheless, he expects to be ready to overthrow Bears receivers by training camp.

—Steve Rosenbloom of the *Chicago Tribune*, on one of the Chicago Bears' backup quarterbacks

He proves it every day in practice by overthrowing receivers.

—Iowa football coach Hayden Fry, on quarterback Mark Vlasic having a stronger arm than his predecessor, Chuck Long

Washington Redskins owner Daniel Snyder had successful surgery to remove a cancerous thyroid and is doing fine, despite the fact that he tried to have the doctor fired halfway through the operation.

—Michael Ventre of msnbc.com

It was gratifying, in a way, to note plastic surgery has been good to at least one member of the Jackson family.

—Greg Cote of the *Miami Herald*, on the incident where Justin Timberlake tore off part of Janet Jackson's top, exposing her right breast during the Super Bowl halftime show

The Raiders have parted ways with Bill Romanowski. Let me guess—pharmaceutical differences?

—Bill Scheft of *Sports Illustrated*, on the pill-popping ex-Oakland linebacker

YOU DON'T SAY!

I lean one way and I'm five eleven. I lean the other way and I'm six feet.

—Joe Thiesmann, on his recovery from a broken leg

After a team doctor gave 49ers tight end Greg Clark an injection and his lung collapsed . . . Good thing Clark wasn't being treated for a groin injury.

—Bob Lacey of the *Half Moon Bay (CA) Review*

You've got to feel all kinds of sorry for Griffey. He remains the only person I've ever heard of who donated his body to science before he was done with it.

—Steve Hummer of the *Atlanta Journal-Constitution*, on the injury woes of Cincinnati Reds outfielder Ken Griffey Jr.

What do steroids and Commissioner Bud Selig have in common? Answer: Both can cause contraction.

—Chris Dufresne of the *Los Angeles Times*

They're worried about catching the SARS virus, but the team doctor cleared them to go. He said after watching them play, he realized these guys can't catch anything.

—Jay Leno, on the dreadful Detroit Tigers visiting Toronto

Give you an idea how long ago they got married—you know where they met? At a Cubs World Series game.

—Jay Leno, after America's longest-married couple celebrated their eighty-first wedding anniversary. He's 100, she's ninety-seven

The Tampa Bay Devil Rays held a special Sunday promotion to take your mother to their game against the Detroit Tigers. Come on, who does that to their own mom?

—Jerry Greene in the *Orlando Sentinel*

The Marlins called three times before he made it to the phone.

—Jim Armstrong of the *Denver Post*, on Florida making seventy-two-year-old Jack McKeon the oldest manager in baseball

Today, he was tossed to the ground by Pedro Martinez.

—*Late Show* host David Letterman, on how the world's oldest man celebrated his 114th birthday, referring to Pedro's head-grab on New York Yankees coach Don Zimmer in the baseball playoffs

I've got a celebrity birthday for you—Angela Lansbury. How many of you love and remember Angela Lansbury from *Murder, She Wrote*? Seventy-eight years old today. As a special treat, Pedro Martinez threw her to the ground.

—David Letterman

I wouldn't make too much because I'm ninety-one years old.

—Buck O'Neil, former Negro League star, when asked how much money he could be making as a player now

I still throw as hard as ever. It just takes twice as long to get there.

—Former pitcher Warren Spahn, on the velocity of his pitches at the age of sixty-seven

Samsonitis.

—Expos publicity director Richard Griffin, explaining an injury diagnosis after Montreal pitcher Dennis Martinez pulled a rib muscle tossing his suitcase onto the team's equipment truck

2000 will be "Y2NoKs" for the Phillies.

—Bill Conlin of the *Philadelphia Inquirer*, on the loss of strikeout pitcher Curt Schilling for several months

Anyone in New York can tell you how hard it is to get through the day in that city without the use of your middle finger.

—Bret Lewis of KFWB in Los Angeles, on New York Mets pitcher Satoru Komiyama being placed on the disabled list after he broke the middle finger on his pitching hand opening a garage door

It was a slider . . . it slid all the way to the on-deck circle.

—Seventy-nine-year-old former *Vancouver Province* writer Clancy Loranger, on tossing out the ceremonial first pitch at Nat Bailey Stadium

Let's get ready to stumble!

—Jay Leno, on the fight between George Foreman, fifty, and Larry Holmes, forty-eight

How come? His thumb go?

—*New York Daily News* columnist Mike Lupica, on the retirement of bowler Earl Anthony

When I saw that bear come smoking down on me, I didn't have any trouble in deciding who was the endangered species.

—Bill Hill, a hunting guide in Montana's Cabinet Mountains, explaining why he and two others had killed a grizzly in a protected area

Tom's manic and I'm depressive, and together we make one healthy person.

—*Sporting Life* cartoonist Ben Templeton, on his symbiotic relationship with partner Tom Forman

After one week, Ben had the kid running a 3.9-second forty-yard dash, bench-pressing 450 pounds, and producing urine that glows in the dark.

—Scott Ostler of the *San Francisco Chronicle*, after Ben Johnson was hired to give sprint lessons to Saad Gadhafi, son of Libyan leader Mu'ammar Muhammad al-Gadhafi

Clean and Jerk.

—Peter Bartlett in the *San Francisco Chronicle*, referring to Marion Jones and then-husband C. J. Hunter, the disgraced shot-putter whose reading for the steroid Nandrolone was 1,000 times over the legal limit

I went to the doctor the other day and told him I had a problem with loss of memory. He asked me how long I've had the problem, and I said, "What problem?"

—Pete Clentzos, a ninety-four-year-old Greek pole-vaulter who competed in the 1932 Olympics, speaking to the *Los Angeles Times*

My arm has felt so bad since I retired that I can't even throw a tantrum.

—Chicago Cubs broadcaster Steve Stone, when asked if he would attempt a Jim Palmer–type comeback

Andre Dawson has a bruised knee and is listed as day-to-day. [Pause] Aren't we all?

—Los Angeles Dodgers broadcaster Vin Scully, during a game against the Chicago Cubs

When Steve and I die, we're going to be buried sixty feet, six inches apart.

—Ex-Phillies catcher Tim McCarver, on his close relationship with pitcher Steve Carlton

When Charlie Finley had his heart operation, it took eight hours—seven just to find his heart.

—Oakland pitcher Steve McCatty, on the As' former owner

SOMEBODY ELSE PUT THEIR FOOT IN MY MOUTH FOR A CHANGE.

—Seattle Mariners outfielder Jay Buhner, after taking a shot to the jaw while breaking up a double play

You need thick skin to play in New York.

—Seattle Mariners first baseman John Olerud, after teammate Bret Boone was stung by a bee at Yankee Stadium

Babe Ruth was voted "the greatest living player" by 1.5 percent of current players polled? I guess Ted Williams got left out in the cold.

—Bob Lacey of *Half Moon Bay (CA) Review*

The prize may go to Clarence "Climax" Blethen. A thirty-year-old Red Sox rookie, Blethen thought he'd look meaner if he took out his false teeth when he pitched and kept them in his hip pocket. Yes, he forgot to put them back in his mouth. So, on September 21, 1923, while sliding into second base, Blethen bit himself in the butt.

—Thomas Boswell of the *Washington Post*, recalling one of the most bizarre injuries in baseball history

Barr, who spent most of his career with the Giants, punched his hand through a paper sign a fan had placed over a toilet seat. Unfortunately, there was wood behind the poster. Barr hurt his pitching hand and missed the playoffs.

—Peter Schmuck of the *Baltimore Sun*, recalling pitcher Jim Barr's celebration of the Angels' division title

5. Ryan Klesko pulling a muscle while picking up a lunch tray
4. Terry Harper dislocating his shoulder in the on-deck circle while waving in a runner on a passed ball
3. Knuckleball pitcher Steve Sparks, emulating a motivational speaker, dislocating his shoulder trying to tear a phone book in half
2. Ex-journeyman reliever Randy Veres hurting his hand while pounding a hotel wall in an attempt to quiet down the loud guests in an adjacent room
1. Braves' John Smoltz scalding his chest while ironing a shirt. Uh, the shirt he happens to be wearing

—John McGrath of the *Tacoma News Tribune*, with his top five bizarre baseball injuries after Sammy Sosa removed himself from the Chicago Cubs lineup after he sneezed and hurt his back

CHAPTER 7

LATE SHIFT

The kings of late-night television have never shied away from poking fun at the world of sports . . . nor should they. There is way too much comedy material in the way pro athletes act, in how much money they rake in, and in the ridiculous statements they often make. From Jay Leno and David Letterman to Conan O'Brien and former *Sportscenter* anchor Craig Kilborn, monologue observations are usually right on the money.

I bought the book, and it was 175 pages. I put it on the table, and the next morning, it was 225 pages.

—Jay Leno, on Jose Canseco's controversial steroid-filled book

Thanks to his $252 million contract, Alex Rodriguez makes $40,000 every time he gets up at bat. In fact, Saturday night when he set his clock ahead, it cost him $28,000.

—Jay Leno

TAXES ARE DUE. TWO WEEKS UNTIL YOUR TAXES ARE DUE. HERE'S A LITTLE TIP. IF YOU OWN CLIPPERS SEASON TICKETS, THEY CAN BE WRITTEN OFF AS A TOTAL LOSS.

—Jay Leno, on Los Angeles's other basketball team

It's been lousy cold lately. Yesterday, it was so cold for opening day at Yankee Stadium that Ted Williams threw out the first pitch.

—David Letterman, on an unusually chilly start to the major league baseball season

The Clippers have provided the only dry spell.

—Jay Leno, talking about the wet weather in Southern California

Boy, is it foggy in Los Angeles. How foggy you ask? Well there's so much fog the L.A. Clippers can't even tell which team they are losing to.

—Jay Leno

In fact, it's so cold back East today, Ted Williams showed up for spring practice.

—Jay Leno, on a cold snap in the weather

I call Los Angeles the city of alternatives. If you don't like mountains, we got the ocean. If you don't like Knotts Berry Farm, we've got Disneyland. If you don't like basketball, we've got the Clippers.

—Former late-night talk show host Arsenio Hall

Over the weekend, the Philadelphia Phillies' Veterans Stadium was blown up. Fans cried because they heard the Phillies weren't in there.

—Craig Kilborn

They might have to call up Winona Ryder from Columbus.

—David Letterman, on the repercussions of the Yankees releasing Ruben Rivera for stealing Derek Jeter's glove and bat

Years ago when you thought of the Yankees, you thought of Whitey Ford. Now, of course, you think of Betty Ford.

—David Letterman, on Dwight Gooden joining Steve Howe and Darryl Strawberry with the Yankees

The New York Yankees are playing great. The people on that team are very optimistic. In fact, Darryl Strawberry is already planning not to report his World Series income.

—David Letterman

A New Jersey man has been sentenced to three years in prison for trying to smuggle cocaine into the country in the belly of an Old English sheepdog. The good news is the dog is fine. The only side effect is, it keeps chasing Dwight Gooden's car.

—David Letterman

If he's convicted, he'll be re-signed by the Yankees.

—David Letterman, on the arrest of former Yankees first baseman Joe Pepitone on a drunk driving charge

Read in the paper today that 80 percent of the world's cocaine is controlled by one drug cartel in Colombia. The other 20 percent is controlled by the Yankees' dugout.

—Jay Leno

Bret Saberhagen, a former New York Met, was traded to the Colorado Rockies. In return, the Mets got two minor leaguers and a substance abuser to be named later.

—David Letterman, on one of baseball's biggest deals

Have you heard about the Pittsburgh Pirates player that hit a mascot with a bat in Milwaukee? The same thing happened with some Mets players, except they swung and missed.

—Conan O'Brien

Watching CNN last night. Unbelievable. More bombings. More shellings. More people getting hurt. But enough about Vince Coleman.

—Jay Leno, on the former New York Mets outfielder

T-ball is just like baseball except there's no pitching—like the New York Mets.

—David Letterman, after the new T-ball field on the White House South Lawn was dedicated, and the first game was played

Here's the latest news about the war. Over the weekend the air force dropped 100,000 leaflets on the Iraqi army telling them that they have no chance of winning. Then today, the air force did the same for the New York Mets.

—Conan O'Brien

In a recent survey, only 13 percent of Americans said that baseball was their favorite sport. The survey was taken in the Mets dugout.

—Conan O'Brien

Here's the sad part—the poll was of the Chicago Bears players.

—Jay Leno, after the National Health Service revealed that 64 percent of men surveyed said they now get exercise

The World Wrestling Federation has lost a judgment over the use of the initials "WWF." After an exhaustive search, they found three initials no one else is using: "XFL."

—Craig Kilborn

This year the Academy assured the Oscars wouldn't be stolen by shipping them in boxes labeled "XFL season tickets."

—Jay Leno

This move could potentially double the number of people who show no interest in the games.

—Dennis Miller, on *Saturday Night Live*, after the World League of American Football announced plans to expand

Watch this show or I might have to go back to football.

—Dennis Miller, promoting his new show on CNBC

There will be no wedding on Saturday. It's a bye week.

—David Letterman, with an update for Britney Spears fans

The Cowboys picked up their fifth ring. Three more, they're tied with Larry King.

—David Letterman

According to a new survey, 60 percent of adults say they're aware of someone who's gone to work under the influence of drugs. Apparently the other 40 percent have never heard of the Dallas Cowboys.

—Conan O'Brien

Each player on the Baltimore Ravens will earn $52,000, or as they call it, "bail."

—Conan O'Brien, on the winner's share for the Super Bowl

The NFL is going to start its own twenty-four-hour cable network featuring players, games, and stats. This is good because up until now the only channel to find twenty-four-hour coverage of NFL players was Court TV.

—Conan O'Brien

Oklahoma's football team has already been ranked tenth in the preseason polls—that's UPI and FBI.

—Jay Leno

Here's some good news. A woman just graduated from the University of Southern Florida at the age of seventy-six. It took her fifty-seven years to finish college. You know what you call people who take fifty-seven years to finish college? Linemen.

—Jay Leno

Did you see him last night at Giants Stadium? That was pretty exciting. My favorite part was when he threw the Hail Mary pass.

—Jay Leno, on Pope John Paul II's visit to the United States

Shaq gets $117 million from the Los Angeles Lakers for four years . . . that works out to $117 million a free throw.

—Jay Leno

It says, "Season's Beatings."

—Jay Leno, on the Christmas card he received from the NBA

Did you know that all the jewelry worn by the actresses was on loan from Kobe Bryant's wife?

—Craig Kilborn, with a fact from Oscars night

I have good news for you Lakers fans. Kobe feels so guilty [about losing the NBA finals to the Detroit Pistons], you're all getting diamond rings.

—Craig Kilborn

She's thirty-eight, he's fifty-four. And you know Phil, he's really comfortable with that sixteen-point lead.

—Jay Leno, on former Los Angeles Lakers coach Phil Jackson, who is dating the daughter of Lakers owner Jerry Buss

They arrested another Hussein half brother today. What is that, like the third half brother so far? They're half brothers and then when they're caught they're quarter brothers. How many half brothers did he have? What, was Hussein's father in the NBA?

—Jay Leno, on capturing Saddam Hussein's family members in Iraq

HE LOOKS SO YOUNG, HE GETS FAN MAIL FROM MICHAEL JACKSON.

—Comedian Billy Crystal, on the Phoenix Suns' Danny Ainge

LeBron James will be playing for the Cleveland Cavaliers. So at least he'll still get to experience what it's like to play on a college team.

—Jay Leno, on the high school phenom selected first in the 2003 NBA draft

We are just about to start March Madness. That's the college basketball tournament where we start with sixty-four teams and whittle them down to just one. You know, kind of like our allies.

—Jay Leno, linking NCAA basketball to U.S. foreign policy

Good news, though. Phil Rizutto went three-for-four.

—David Letterman, on the opening of the exhibition season with replacement players

They showed one guy who went to grab his crotch and missed.

—Jay Leno, on replacement players not up to major-league quality

Having Jay Leno sing "Take Me Out to the Ballgame" at Wrigley Field certainly gives new meaning to the phrase "chin music."

—Jeff Schnurbusch in the *St. Louis Post-Dispatch*

Take your daughter to work day is coming up soon, April 26. Finally, a chance for the Detroit Tigers to win a game.

—Jay Leno

Hookers today in Times Square are offering their "Cal Ripken Jr. Special." For $25, you can keep going as long as you're physically able.

—David Letterman

Baseball all-star game canceled . . . no steroids available.

—Headline from NBC's *Tonight Show*

Today Major League Baseball announced they will conduct mandatory testing for steroids next season after more than 5 percent of the players tested positive this year. Do you know what they call the 5 percent of the players who tested positive? The all-stars.

—Jay Leno

According to rumors, Saddam is being hidden by relatives in his hometown. No, wait a minute—that's the Chicago Cubs fan.

—David Letterman, on the whereabouts of Saddam Hussein

You know they went through sixty athletes in one night. That hasn't been done since Madonna's last world tour.

—Jay Leno, on the Major League Baseball All-Star game, which ended in a tie

Did you hear about that amazing play Mondesi made against the Padres? Apparently he got the guy at the plate on a throw from the bar across the street.

—Jay Leno, talking about Los Angeles Dodgers outfielder Raul Mondesi, after facing an impaired-driving charge

Rush Limbaugh donated all his leftover painkillers to the city of Boston, and there was enough for everybody.

—Jay Leno, with good news for formerly cursed Red Sox fans

The stadium was packed because it was J.Lo's ex-husband day.

—*Late Night* host Conan O'Brien, after Jennifer Lopez and Ben Affleck were seen together at a Boston Red Sox game

Say what you will about President Clinton, he is a pretty shrewd man. Clinton is now telling close friends and associates that he and Monica Lewinsky were practicing for the two-man luge.

—David Letterman

The big news from Major League Baseball is that Hillary Clinton will throw out the first ball at a Chicago Cubs game. Here in L.A., finding a celebrity to throw out the first ball is not a problem. The hard part is finding a Dodger who can catch it.

—Jay Leno

The latest big news is that Greece may not finish some of the buildings needed for the [Olympic] Games. In a related story, this year the triathlon will consist of running, swimming, and concrete pouring.

—Conan O'Brien

According to *Men's Health* magazine the best place to meet women is at art museums. The worst place to meet women—Augusta National Golf Course.

—Jay Leno

A Wisconsin man was cited for drunk driving after he crashed his golf cart into a highway road marker. The guy was driving his golf cart down the highway! Forget the drinking for a minute. How bad a golfer was this guy?

—Jay Leno

Lance Armstrong is getting a divorce. That's sad. Divorce! Now he'll really be riding a bike everywhere.

—Jay Leno, on the Tour de France cycling champ

What am I going to do with that extra minute?

—David Letterman, upset with the cancellation of the Mike Tyson–Buster Mathis Jr. fight

It was announced that Mike Tyson's next fight will be on regular television instead of pay-per-view. It will air on November 4 from 9:00 to 9:01.

—Conan O'Brien

What do you think this kid's life is gonna be like when he gets older? "Hey, my dad can eat your dad."

—Jay Leno, on Mike Tyson's wife giving birth to a baby boy

Joe Used to Be a Millionaire.

—Jay Leno, proposing a reality television show featuring Mike Tyson

This is the first match where you could suffer brain damage just by watching the fight.

—Jay Leno, on the Paula Jones–Tonya Harding boxing exhibition

The new heavyweight champion of the world, Hasim Rahman, took a vow of poverty. It's not religious. He signed with Don King.

—Jay Leno

CHAPTER 8

AND NOW, A WORD FROM OUR SPONSORS

Some say it began during the 1984 Summer Olympics in Los Angeles. "This bathroom break is brought to you by . . . " Commercialism and sport now go hand-in-money-grubbing-hand, a fact of life at any stadium, arena, or park. From the breaks during televised games to the placement of corporate logos, it's impossible to watch a professional sporting event without being bombarded with sponsorships. Don't think the athletes haven't noticed.

That's like having Miller Lite and AA.

—Golfer John Daly, on an endorsement portfolio that includes TrimSpa and Dunkin' Donuts

Tickets are now on sale for the World Figure Skating Championships at the MCI Center. For an additional $5, they'll tell you who's going to win.

—Dan Daly of the *Washington Times*

Check this one out: Cardinal Health Incorporated is the official supplier of medical supplies and drugs to the Salt Lake City Olympics. Its pharmacy services manager is Ben Johnson.

—Jim Melidones in the *San Francisco Chronicle*

Olympic skiing hero Picabo Street will donate a share of her endorsement earnings to fund a new wing of a Denver hospital. In return, the hospital will name the facility after her. It'll be called Picabo I.C.U.

—Overheard on the streets in Denver

I look forward to the day when they drop all pretenses and replace the water in the Olympic swimming pool with Sprite.

—Tony Kornheiser of the *Washington Post*, on corporate sponsorships at the Summer Olympic Games

Not sure who No. 1 is, but if those plastic bags with brewskis he carried from the clubhouse as a Blue Jay were any indication, we're guessing it's David Wells.

—Bill Lankhof of the *Toronto Sun*, on Coors and Molson merging to become the No. 2 brewery in the world

Now that Coors sponsors the Heisman Trophy, will there be a separate Heisman Light for small schools?

—Greg Cote of the *Miami Herald*

One time I lost my substitute urine when I got stoned and dropped my Gatorade bottle, so I called a girlfriend and asked her for a favor. She Fed-Exed me a urine sample, but I failed the test because I came up pregnant.

—Former Carolina Panthers defensive end Shawn King, on failing an NFL drug test

If I'm Dusty Baker and the Cubs win the World Series, I'm making darn sure that's Gatorade the players are pouring on me.

—Jim Armstrong of the *Denver Post,* after Chicago Cubs outfielder Moises Alou admitted that he uses urine on his hands to toughen up his skin

It was on at 5 A.M., and I was having a great time. I'm sitting there in my underwear, having a beer, and the next thing I know they come over and finally toss me out of Hooters.

—David Letterman, on the Yankees–Devil Rays season opener in Japan

Until an outcry forced cancellation of the promotion, the minor-league Charleston [South Carolina] RiverDogs planned Free Vasectomy Day to coincide with Father's Day. The outfielders had been instructed, "Whatever you do, don't hit the cut-off man."

—Comedian Argus Hamilton

Veeck also held other outlandish promotions like "Tonya Harding bat day" and "Vasectomy night," although that was nipped at the last minute.

—Steve Rosenbloom of the *Chicago Tribune*, after Charleston Riverdogs owner Mike Veeck held a "nobody night" promotion

To which representatives of the Montreal Expos replied, "Hey, get your own idea. We're working this side of the street, pal!"

—Comedian Alex Kaseberg, on the minor-league Charleston RiverDogs no-fans allowed promotion

Albert Belle Slugger Cereal, named for the volatile Orioles slugger, will be marketed in the Baltimore area. It's an eighteen-ounce box of corn flakes. They don't crackle or pop—they just snap.

—Comedian Argus Hamilton

Since Disney owns Winnie the Pooh, Woods has changed his name to Tigger.

—Keith Olbermann of Fox Sports Net, on Tiger Woods signing a sponsorship deal with Disney

We're in the hole.

—Comedian Alan Ray, suggesting a new marketing slogan for Top-Flite after the golf ball maker filed for bankruptcy

Wife Amy better hope Phil doesn't win the John Deere Classic. It'll get awfully crowded in the sack with Phil, Amy, and a riding lawnmower.

—Mike Bianchi of the *Orlando Sentinel*, after Phil Mickelson wore his green jacket to bed after winning the 2004 Masters

I was really going to retire, but Mr. Visa and Mr. American Express told me I better stick around another year.

—NBA center Joe Kleine, on why he returned for a final season with Portland

Whoever stole it is spending less money than my wife.

—Former tennis bad boy Ilie Nastase, on why he never reported his missing American Express credit card

We never leave home without him.

—Philadelphia Flyers coach Bill Dineen, after his son, Kevin Dineen of the Flyers, was named American Express man of the year

Hey, I'm already at Disneyland.

—Angels outfielder Tim Salmon, possibly envisioning a World Series MVP speech, on the downside of his team's location

We're really pleased. This is the highest the Mariners have ever finished.

—Chuck Armstrong, the Seattle Mariners chief operating officer, on the organization's placing third in a local corporate spelling bee

You mix two jiggers of Scotch to one jigger of Metrecal. So far I've lost five pounds and my driver's license.

—Former Cincinnati Reds infielder Rocky Bridges, on his diet

Sounds like he's been flying United to me.

—Jay Leno, on the news that Florida Marlins outfielder Andre Dawson, who pays child support to a Delta Air Lines reservationist for their seven-year-old daughter, is now being sued for child support by a USAir flight attendant for their six-year-old son

This makes the SkyDome restaurant the only place in town where the waiter considers it a compliment when someone points out that "there's a fly in my soup."

—Bill Lankhof of the *Toronto Sun*, after Carlos Delgado hit a record-tying four home runs in a game against Tampa, one of which struck the Windows eatery beyond center field

Because they play at Enron Field, this might be a good time for the Houston Astros to claim their record in the postseason is the result of accounting errors.

—Michael Ventre of msnbc.com

The San Diego Padres' new ballpark will be called Petco Park, after the animal-supply company agreed to a twenty-two-year lease for naming rights. The Padres hope the new park will give them a leg up on the National League West.

—Dwight Perry of the *Seattle Times*

3Com Park is the worst place to watch a major league baseball game since Candlestick Park.

—Allan Malamud of the *Los Angeles Times*

IT'S THE ONLY PARK AROUND WHERE THEY CAN HAVE A SEVENTH-INNING FETCH.

—Los Angeles Dodgers broadcaster Vin Scully, on the fact that Portuguese water dogs retrieve home-run balls from McCovey Cove at San Francisco's Pacific Bell Park

They were going to have the Little League World Series at Coors Field, but they decided the fences were too close.

—Bob Kravitz of Denver's *Rocky Mountain News*

Devil Rays home attendance has dropped every season, to last year's average of 13,070 per game, and most of those people wandered into Tropicana Field accidentally [while] looking for a Wal-Mart.

—Syndicated columnist Norman Chad

If they had any sense of humor, they would stretch a tarp across it with the words: "Less Filling."

—Bill Scheft of *Sports Illustrated*, on the Milwaukee Brewers thinking about closing the upper deck at Miller Park

Who let the dog in?

—A sign up in Seattle upon the return of Alex Rodriguez, known as Pay-Rod at Safeco Field

The Intentional Wok.

—ESPN announcers, describing the Chinese food concession at Seattle's Safeco Field during an A's–Mariners game

Unsafeco Field.

—Steve Rushin of *Sports Illustrated*, on the San Quentin Giants, a baseball team of convicts, hosting the semipro Novato Knicks at the California prison

Cute story. Detroit parents Nick and Sarah Arena name their newborn son Joe Louis Arena. My wife is expecting quads. We've decided to name them Fenway, Roland Garros, Minute Maid, and Network Associates.

—Scott Ostler of the *San Francisco Chronicle*

How about special discount seats for seniors called, "The obituary section"?

—Bill Conlin of the *Philadelphia Daily News*, after the *St. Petersburg Times* newspaper bought the naming rights to the Tampa Bay Lightning's arena

We'd feel a lot better if you took us to Toys "R" Us.

—Six-year-old McKenzie MacLean, upon hearing that her dad, Doug MacLean, had been dismissed as coach of the Florida Panthers

Is this why, in all those Lays potato-chip commercials, Mark Messier keeps saying, "Betcha can't eat just one"?

—Randy Turner of the *Winnipeg Free Press*, after a woman in Des Moines, Iowa, reportedly found marijuana in her bag of Uncle Ray's munchies

Joe Gold, founder of Gold's Gym and World Gym, has passed away at eighty-two. The funeral took longer than normal. Pallbearers lowered him into the ground with three sets of ten.

—Comedian Alan Ray

Truly a player to be named later.

—*San Francisco Chronicle* columnist Tom FitzGerald, on Steffi Graf and Andre Agassi expecting a baby, and the promoter of a New Jersey tennis tournament willing to give a $10 million guarantee to the child to appear in his event in 2017

I walked about ten feet, and the shoes had a message for me: "Lie down."

—Jerry Greene in the *Orlando Sentinel*, on taking a pair of $250 Adidas "smart shoes" for a test

With Nextel replacing Winston as sponsor of NASCAR's top series, there goes the TV announcers' excuse that "this race is just too close to call."

—Dwight Perry of the *Seattle Times*

I just got back from court where I had my name officially changed to Willy T. McRibbs.

—Willy T. Ribbs, the first black to qualify for the Indy 500, on McDonald's decision to sponsor his car

The ceremony was supposed to take place at the start of the season, but it took five months to let the ring out a couple of sizes.

—Bill Scheft of *Sports Illustrated*, after the Phoenix Suns put Charles Barkley in their Ring of Honor

If the network pushes it to a thirty-minute halftime in Game 5, I wouldn't be surprised if it showed us a few more events from the 2000 Summer Olympics.

—Syndicated columnist Norman Chad, on the lengthy NBA finals halftimes breaks that were lasting in excess of twenty-three minutes in the first four games

We want to show that Utah is more than Karl Malone, beautiful mountains, and some guy with five wives and twenty-six kids.

—Bob Costas of NBC, on coverage of the Salt Lake City Winter Olympics

He's finally getting a chance to interview someone his own size.

—Columnist Geno Zertuche, on Costas doing play-by-play for the first T-ball game on the White House lawn

The problem that Gibbs faces is that he'll be coaching at FedEx Field, where change is expected to arrive overnight.

—Randy Hill of foxsports.com, after Joe Gibbs returned to coach the Washington Redskins despite being out of the business for a dozen years

Which game gets to your house first—the Domino's Pizza Copper Bowl or the Federal Express Orange Bowl?

—Mike Littman, *Baltimore Evening Sun* columnist, on the college bowl games

I said some people don't know a football from a banana . . . The next morning a local banana distributor sent me a huge crate of bananas. This week I'm going to say, "some people don't know a football from a Mercedes."

—Former Tampa Bay and USC football coach John McKay

During halftime of an XFL game, NBC cameras "walked in on an unidentified man using a urinal"—maybe, just maybe, it was Vince McMahon watching the league's future.

—*USA Today*

Every single ad was based on some sort of dumb animal—be it a bear, pig, cow, or supermodel.

—Comedian Kathleen Madigan, on Super Bowl commercials

The only time they ever called me was when they wanted to know if I would renew my subscription.

—Former Canadian Football League offensive lineman-turned-commentator Chris Walby, on Hamilton Tiger Cats receiver Darren Flutie being sought by *Sports Illustrated* for a feature

Sports Illustrated managing editor Bill Colson has been asked to cut 8 percent of his $50 million annual budget, according to *Adweek*. You know what that means—even skimpier swimsuits next February.

—Tom FitzGerald of the *San Francisco Chronicle*

CHAPTER 9

FINANCIAL TIMES

Money makes the sports world go around—from fat contracts, to owners rich enough to treat their pro franchises like an expensive, ego-driven hobby, to labor disputes, some of the best laughs in sports have come out of the tension that builds during arguments about money. Adding to the humor is the massive increase in ticket prices within the past decade, a necessary evil to make up for those hefty contracts.

Problem is, they're playing in all of them.

—Larry Brooks of the *New York Post*, on the ten high priced "premium games" on the New York Islanders' schedule

Maybe he saw our new ticket prices.

—Atlanta Hawks president Stan Kasten, on a mugger who attacked him

Cheapest average ticket in baseball is $9 American for the Expos, but plane fare to Puerto Rico is not included.

—Jerry Greene in the *Orlando Sentinel*, on the Montreal Expos

The Montreal Expos have announced practices will be closed to the public. They want to simulate a real game atmosphere.

—Alan Ray in the *San Francisco Chronicle*

The minority owners of the Expos are suing commissioner Bud Selig under the Racketeer Influenced and Corruption Organizations act. This makes Selig sound like a gangster, which is an insult to gangsters everywhere.

—Steve Rosenbloom of the *Chicago Tribune*

She is now.

—Former Pittsburgh Pirates manager Chuck Tanner, when asked if his aunt who won $2.5 million in a lottery was his favorite aunt

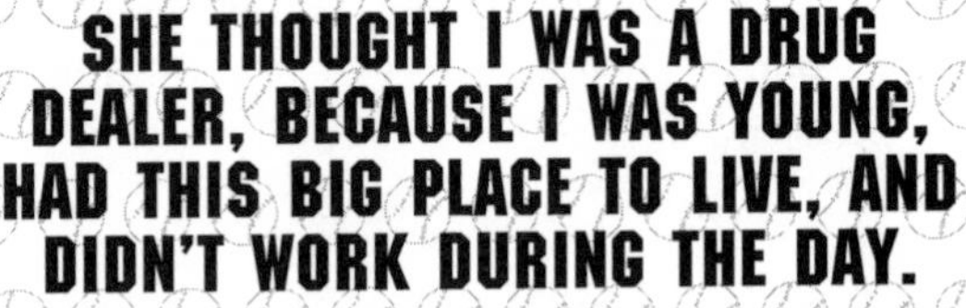

SHE THOUGHT I WAS A DRUG DEALER, BECAUSE I WAS YOUNG, HAD THIS BIG PLACE TO LIVE, AND DIDN'T WORK DURING THE DAY.

—Cleveland Indians pitcher Terry Mulholland, on the first impression he made on his future wife

Just a couple of million more than you.

—Pete Rose in the *Los Angeles Times*, after former Los Angeles Dodger Steve Garvey asked him how much money Rose would be making if he were playing today

That's like Al Capone speaking out for gun control.

—*Dallas Morning News* columnist Blackie Sherrod, on the complaint by Atlanta Braves owner Ted Turner that baseball salaries are too high

Jane Fonda and Ted Turner are separating but neither will ask for a divorce. Both are afraid they might be awarded custody of John Rocker.

—Bob Lacey, *Half Moon Bay (CA) Review*

Keeping up with the Joneses has never been tougher.

—Tom FitzGerald of the *San Francisco Chronicle*, after Atlanta Braves standout Chipper Jones bought a new 4,200-acre ranch in Texas that has twelve lakes, seventy-five miles of fence, a 10,000-square-foot home, two guest houses, and a four-hole golf course

St. Louis Cardinals reliever Rich Batchelor will earn $157,500 this season and is married.

—*Sports Illustrated*

A-Rod makes three times as much money as any other Texas Ranger. If his teammates start borrowing money from him, will they call him the Loan Ranger [from the Lone Star State]?

—Steve Abney in the *San Francisco Chronicle*

I'm planning to file for disability on the basis of my long-time allegiance to the Boston Red Sox.

—Barb Lagowski, author of eleven books, including fiction, nonfiction, and humor—before the Red Sox ended the Curse of the Bambino in 2004

A successful bettor has knowledge, patience, selectivity, willpower, and a rich wife.

—Las Vegas oddsmaker Bob Martin

Kind of reminds you of the quote from Zsa Zsa Gabor: "I'm a marvelous housekeeper. Every time I leave a man, I keep his house."

—Mike Bianchi of the *Orlando Sentinel*, on NASCAR driver Jeff Gordon's slump being attributed to his impending divorce and his wife threatening to take their $10 million Palm Beach mansion

When Cochran tries to play the race card this time, it will take on a whole new meaning.

—Mike Bianchi, on O. J. Simpson attorney Johnnie Cochran's threat to sue NASCAR for engaging in unfair business practices

I spent a lot of my money on booze, birds, and fast cars. The rest I just squandered.

—Soccer great George Best

I'm not sure how it works, but judging by Dennis, I think the side effects are pink and green hair.

—Jay Leno, after Dennis Rodman appeared on the *Tonight Show* plugging a sexual-enhancement product

Gary Payton wanted a situation where a group of guys play as a unit with no concern for their own personal glory, but then the Lakers' offer came through.

—Comedian Allan Ray

The British tabloids claim that soccer hunk David Beckham cheated on his wife, Victoria. They may have something. Today Beckham called Kobe Bryant to get the number of his jeweler.

—Comedian Alex Kaseberg

Or as they refer to such a bauble in the NBA: a Kobe Bryant starter kit.

—Randy Turner of the *Winnipeg Free Press*, on reports the Mets' Mike Piazza bought his fiancée a $500,000 engagement ring

Did you hear Kobe is staying? Staying with the Lakers? He decided to stay with the Lakers out of loyalty. You can understand why. The last time he wasn't loyal to someone, it cost him four million bucks in jewelry.

—Jay Leno, on Kobe Bryant re-signing with the L.A. Lakers

It was the first time in my life I was happy to see a zero after my name.

—Tom McMillan, Maryland Democrat and former NBA player, after he was absolved of wrongdoing in the House banking scandal

One of the prizes given away by the team on fan appreciation night was passes to attend a Warriors practice next season. So, there's good news for you, Warrior fans: Next season your team is going to practice.

—Scott Ostler of the *San Francisco Chronicle*, on the dreadful 21-61 Golden State Warriors

They say talk is cheap. That isn't necessarily true.

—Houston forward Charles Barkley, after the NBA fined him $10,000 for ripping referee Jack Nies

The reality is that all TV ratings for shows across the board are down, unless you're getting the opportunity to marry a millionaire, become a millionaire, or watch millionaires wrestle.

—NBA commissioner David Stern, on declining TV ratings

What do you have when you've got an agent buried up to his neck in sand? Not enough sand.

—Pat Williams, Orlando Magic general manager, following a contract hassle with holdout Brian Williams

Anyone else remember when the only labor issues facing the WNBA involved Sheryl Swoopes having a baby?

—Jeff McDonald of the *San Angelo Standard Times*, on the near strike in the WNBA

I saw a quarter, a nickel, and a dime. I could have made forty cents, but it probably would have been an NCAA violation.

—UCLA Bruins basketball player Jason Kapono, after Arizona State fans threw coins on the court during a loss to UCLA

No question, when it comes to track, there are pros and cons.

—Former world shot-put record holder Brian Oldfield, on pro athletes who earn money openly and amateurs who earn it secretly

In keeping with the spirit of NBC's approach to covering the Olympics, this just in: Mark Spitz wins his seventh gold.

—Paola Boivin of the *Arizona Republic*

We also slice men.

—A sign outside a women's hair salon at the Nagano Olympics, which appears to have been lost in the translation

When Chicago's storied NFL franchise sold presenting rights to its team name—as in "Bears football presented by Bank One" for the next twelve years—it left a few unanswered questions. As in: Considering Chicago's 4–12 record last season, is there a more apt nickname in sports than the "B. O. Bears"? Will the team's most coveted product endorser play right guard? And, is anybody doing more revolutions per minute in their grave right now than George Halas?

—Dwight Perry of the *Seattle Times*

They tell me he is so stingy he has a burglar alarm on his garbage can.

—Marv Levy of Fox Sports Net, on Jacksonville Jaguars defensive coordinator Dom Capers

There were 150 people in the courtroom—third-largest crowd ever to see the USFL in action.

—David Letterman, on the USFL antitrust lawsuit against the NFL

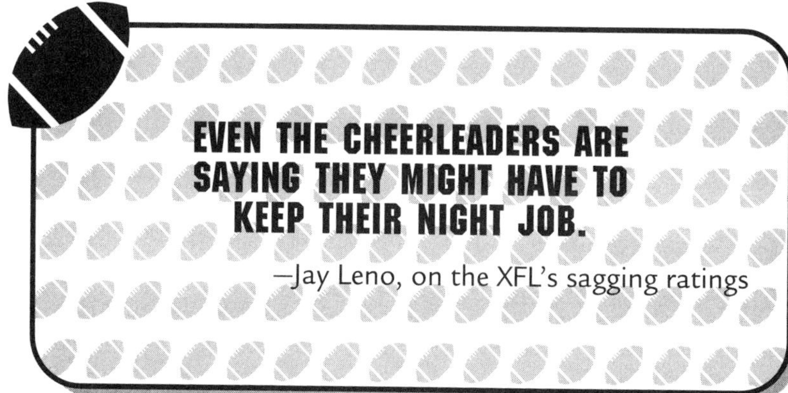

EVEN THE CHEERLEADERS ARE SAYING THEY MIGHT HAVE TO KEEP THEIR NIGHT JOB.

—Jay Leno, on the XFL's sagging ratings

YOU DON'T SAY!

One day, I was standing outside my apartment and, can you believe it, a bum came up and gave me a dollar.

—*Monday Night Football* commentator John Madden, about his casual wardrobe

I'm about to become the first football player to collect his salary and pension at the same time.

—Forty-seven-year-old punter Bob Cameron, after signing a two-year contract extension with the CFL's Winnipeg Blue Bombers

Ryan Leaf threw fourteen touchdown passes in his NFL career and grossed $13 million. Bust? Hardly. I'd say he got the most out of his abilities.

—Mike Bianchi

There hasn't been a bust this expensive since the San Diego Chargers signed Ryan Leaf.

—Cam Hutchinson of the *Saskatoon StarPhoenix*, after twenty CBS stations were fined a total of $550,000 for airing the Janet Jackson breast incident during the infamous Super Bowl halftime show

My family was so poor, my sister was made in Japan.

—Pro golfer Lee Trevino

That bag looks pink to you, but it looks green to me . . . I get $200,000 to use it.

—Senior golfer Chi Chi Rodriguez, on his pink golf bag

When you retire, your wife gets twice as much husband and half as much money. I have to keep playing.

—Chi Chi Rodriguez, on the reason he still played pro golf well into his sixties

The Bruins throw five million bucks his way and he responds with seventeen points and a minus-eighteen rating . . . this begs the question, why isn't he a New York Ranger?

—Elliott Pap of the *Vancouver Sun*, on the Boston Bruins signing forward Martin Lapointe

No, the owners took it all.

—New York Rangers forward Nick Kypreos, asked by custom officials if he had anything to declare upon reentering the United States after the NHL lockout ended

The U.S. Mint said it is sending new-look nickels to the Federal Reserve. So there you go. The Hawks are ready for free agency.

—Steve Rosenbloom in the *Chicago Tribune*, on the penny-pinching Chicago Blackhawks

My wife made me a millionaire. I used to have 3 million.

—Bobby Hull, on his divorce

I'm not a millionaire. It's my ex-wife who's a millionaire.

—Relief pitcher Rollie Fingers, on his thoughts of making a comeback

Major league baseball players have set a strike date of August 30. The pitching staff of the Tampa Bay Devil Rays, however, immediately broke ranks, saying they have every intention of throwing one way before then.

—Scott Feschuk of the *National (Toronto) Post*

More than 735,000 people signed up Friday in the first seventeen hours for the Federal Trade Commission's "do not call" program designed to fend off telemarketers, the FTC announced. And major-league general managers couldn't be happier to join them: No more dinnertime phone calls from Rickey Henderson's agent!

—Dwight Perry of the *Seattle Times*

He's right. The technical term is arson.

—Scott Ostler of the *San Francisco Chronicle*, after Milwaukee Brewers general manager Doug Melvin, trying to rid the team of Richie Sexson's and Geoff Jenkins' $8 million-a-year contracts, declared the move "isn't a fire sale"

I'M RICH. WHAT AM I SUPPOSED TO DO, HIDE IT?

—Detroit Tiger Lou Whitaker, arriving in a stretch limo for a players' union meeting during the baseball strike

I told [general manager] Roland Hemond to go out and get me a big-name pitcher. He said, "Dave Wehrmeister's got eleven letters. Is that a big enough name for you?"

—Eddie Eichorn, Chicago White Sox owner

I am the most loyal player money can buy.

—Don Sutton, pitcher for the Los Angeles Dodgers, Houston Astros, Milwaukee Brewers, Oakland Athletics, and California Angels

People think we make $3 million and $4 million a year. They don't realize that most of us only make $500,000.

—Major league baseball player Pete Incaviglia

I'm just making a visit to my money.

—Marge Schott, former Cincinnati Reds owner, as she was about to travel to Plant City, Florida

I watched CBS. I felt sorry for them losing $95 million on baseball.

—Pittsburgh Pirates outfielder Andy Van Slyke, on what he did during the off-season

Sometimes I get the feeling I'm going to aberration hearings instead of arbitration hearings.

—Pittsburgh Pirates general manager Larry Doughty

I was once offered $300 to throw a fight in the third round but I had to turn it down because I had never made it to the third round.

—Former major-league broadcaster Lon Simmons, reflecting on a very short career as a pro boxer

Tommy squeezes a nickel so tight the Indian sits on a buffalo.

—Irving Rudd, boxing promoter, needling Thomas Hearns about his frugality

He's so broke, his next face tattoo has to be in red ink.

—Bill Scheft of *Sports Illustrated*, on boxer Mike Tyson filing for bankruptcy

Hell, for that money, Leon will come to your house.

—Ferdie Pacheco, the "fight doctor" of NBC, when informed that videocassettes of Leon Spinks' two bouts with Muhammad Ali were selling for $89.95

Just a hunch, but I'm guessing naked tennis is a game of bounces.

—Bob Florence of the *Saskatoon StarPhoenix*, after plans for the first online pay-per-view nude tennis tournament went awry when insufficient software and high traffic volume combined to crash the Florida nudist colony's Web site

I think the first thing [my dad] ever bought me was a football. And I was very young. He didn't know a lot about it. He came from the old country. I mean, we tried to pass it and throw it and kick it, and we couldn't do it. And it was very discouraging for him and for me. We almost quit. And finally we had a nice enough neighbor who came over and put some air in it, and what a difference.

—Milwaukee Brewers broadcaster Bob Uecker, recalling part of his acceptance speech when inducted into the Baseball Hall of Fame

CHAPTER 10

THE COACH APPROACH

The daily duties of a coach or manager include fielding questions from the media, and sometimes a little creative answering can shift the monotony. The most creative people who successfully lead the men and women of sports have found the way to keep reporters on their toes and off the coaches' backs, by making interesting statements and tossing in some spice. They've even found a way to keep things in perspective when the inevitable "Trumping" happens—you're fired.

Is that your final answer?

—What Oakland Raiders defensive coordinator Willie Shaw said to Al Davis after being fired

The guy in front of us is wearing a T-shirt that says, "Good coaches win, great coaches cover."

—T. J. Simers of the *Los Angeles Times*, on betting in Las Vegas for the NCAA men's basketball tournament

Coach Del Harris was given his pink slip, and coincidentally as he was going out the door, Dennis Rodman was coming in wearing his pink slip. So it works out perfectly.

—Jay Leno, on the Los Angeles Lakers

We need a Denise Rodman.

—Stanford women's basketball coach Tara VanDerveer, bemoaning her team's lack of consistent rebounding

I know drugs are a problem in sports. I played football in high school and they were then. I remember the homecoming game—drugs all through the locker room—a guy comes up to me before the game and says, "Dan, I am so wasted. I can't go out there, man." And I said, "Hey, you gotta go out there. We can't play without you, coach."

—Comic Dan Wedeking

I was shocked and surprised . . . I don't know how we scored a run.

—Eric Dennis, Athletic Director at Robert Morris College in Chicago, on how he felt when his school's baseball team lost 71–1 to St. Francis of Illinois

I knew I was in for a long year when we lined up for the national anthem on opening day and one of my players said, "Every time I hear that song I have a bad game."

—Jim Leyland, Pittsburgh Pirates manager

We still go out dining and dancing three times a week. She goes on Mondays, Wednesdays, and Fridays, I go on Tuesdays, Thursdays, and Saturdays.

—Former Los Angeles Dodgers manager Tommy Lasorda, on his long marriage

Yeah, but I love you more than football and basketball.

—Tommy Lasorda, on what he told his wife when she claimed he loved baseball and the Dodgers more than he loved her

When I asked, "How would you like to be married to a major-league manager?" my wife said, "What, is Tommy Lasorda getting a divorce?"

—John Wathan, upon being named Kansas City Royals manager

I've never criticized my players in public, and I'll never do it again.

—New York Mets manager Bobby Valentine

You just listen to the ball and bat come together. They make an awful noise.

—Darrell Johnson, Seattle Mariners manager, on when to change pitchers

There'll be two buses leaving the hotel for the park tomorrow. The two o'clock bus will be for those of you who need a little extra work. The empty bus will be leaving at five o'clock.

—San Francisco Giants manager Dave Bristol, addressing his struggling team

We had our father-son game the other day. Our guys thought they were supposed to call their fathers to come in for the game.

—Pittsburgh Pirates coach Rich Donnelly, on his youthful team

In Cleveland, pennant fever usually ends up being just a forty-eight-hour virus.

—Frank Robinson, on his first managerial job with the Indians

It's a good thing Norfolk Tides center fielder Esix Snead doesn't play shortstop. His first name, E-six, is a manager's nightmare.

—Bob Molinaro of the *Norfolk Virginian-Pilot*

Swingley is so good at managing a bunch of dogs, they're thinking of making him manager of the Chicago Cubs.

—Comedy writer Alex Kaseberg, after Doug Swingley's dogsled team won its third consecutive Iditarod race

Baseball fans in New York have black teeth, their breath smells like beer, and they have nicknames such as Greasy, Scarface, and Toothless. And the men are even worse.

—Former Utah Jazz coach Frank Layden, on growing up in New York

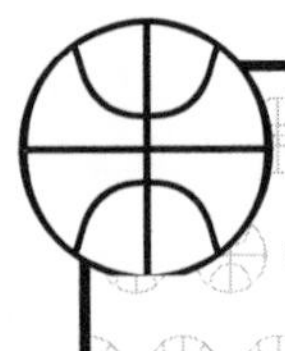

IT'S KIND OF TOUGH GOING TO PRACTICE AND YOU'RE SUPPOSED TO BE THE COACH AND YOU'RE THE DUMBEST ONE THERE.

—Tom Murphy, basketball coach at academically oriented Hamilton College

When I coached at Marquette, I told the players we go first class. We don't take the towels from the hotel rooms. We take the television sets.

—Al McGuire

We're so young, we've decided to dress only seven players on the road. We're pretty confident the other five can dress themselves.

—Charlie Just, women's basketball coach at Bellarmine College in Louisville, on his team's inexperience

That was some of the worst fun I ever had.

—Longmont (Colorado) High School basketball coach Bob Betz, following a loss

When the athletic director said I should recruit more whites to keep the folks in Pullman happy, I signed Rufus White and Willie White.

—George Ravelling, Washington State basketball coach, after it was suggested he should recruit more white players to Pullman, Washington

If you went to my school with two ears, it was obvious you were a transfer student.

—George Ravelling, recalling his youth in a ghetto in Washington, D.C.

My last season there was reviewed in *Field and Stream*.

—George Ravelling, as the basketball coach at Iowa, on the remoteness of Washington State, where he had coached previously

We're not eating, we're not sleeping. We're like Gandhi.

—Pete Gillen, Xavier University basketball coach, before a game with rival Cincinnati

They asked me to spell Mississippi. I said, "Which one? The state or the river?"

—Pete Gillen, on taking a spelling test to get into college

I have three-point shooters. I just wish I had three-point scorers.

—Dallas Mavericks coach Dick Motta, on his team's poor shooting from three-point range

It was so small we didn't have a village idiot. My brother and I had to take turns.

—Dick Motta, on his hometown of Union, Utah

Losing wasn't a disaster. Getting home after a game and finding no scotch in the liquor cabinet—that was a disaster.

—Former Knicks coach Red Holzman, on his days in the NBA

I don't have an ulcer. I'm a carrier. I give them to other people.

—Cleveland Cavaliers coach Bill Fitch

We're the only team in history that could lose nine games in a row and then go into a slump.

—Bill Fitch, in his first season of coaching the Cavaliers

My daughter was a little worried. She wondered if I'd go after Barney.

—Edmonton Oilers coach Craig MacTavish, reflecting on the fallout from his run-in with Calgary Flames mascot Harvey the Hound

I don't even want to guess where that puck finally ended up. Only Tommy can answer that.

—Craig MacTavish, after a Minnesota Wild shot wound up in the pants of Edmonton Oilers goaltender Tommy Salo

He's the only guy in the league with an autographed copy of the Bible.

—James Cybulski of The Score TV Network (Canada), on sixty-seven-year-old Calgary Flames interim head coach Al McNeil

They took an X-ray and didn't find anything.

—New Jersey Devils coach Larry Robinson, on whether Jason Arnott, woozy after he took a puck to the head, would suit up for the next game

Larry Robinson withdrew as a candidate to coach the New York Rangers. Apparently he'd like an easier challenge. Like rebuilding Iraq.

—Bill Scheft of *Sports Illustrated*

You hated him for 364 days a year. And on the 365th day you collected your Stanley Cup rings.

—Ex-Montreal Canadien Steve Shutt, on playing for, and winning five titles with, coach Scotty Bowman

After her conviction, Marie Antoinette was paraded in the back of a cart among the mobs lining the streets of Paris. She was taken to the guillotine on October 16, 1793. There, she suffered an upper-body injury.

—Rich Hofmann, of the *Philadelphia Inquirer*, on the way NHL injuries are described during the Stanley Cup playoffs

Kurt Russell recognized my talent more than Herb did.

—John Harrington, a forward on the 1980 U.S. gold-medal hockey team coached by Herb Brooks, on getting more power-play time in the movie *Miracle* than he did during the Olympics

The thing that I've noticed so far in the playoffs is the better he plays, the bigger they get.

—Anaheim Mighty Ducks coach Mike Babcock, on suggestions that goalie Jean-Sebastien Giguere wears oversized goalie pads

The first goal is important if we get it. If they do, it's not important at all.

—Mike Babcock, on the importance of scoring first

Last season we couldn't win at home, and this season we can't win on the road. My failure as a coach is that I can't think of anyplace else to play.

—Harry Neale, Vancouver Canucks coach, describing the difficulty of his job

McCaskill plays hockey like he pitches—once every four games.

—Winnipeg coach Barry Long, on Kirk McCaskill, who gave up a hockey career with the Jets to become a baseball pitcher

After all these years in the league, am I that stupid that I would put four forwards and one defenseman in a 3–3 tie, in the third period? I think everybody that knows me here knows I'm not that stupid. I might be halfway stupid, but not that stupid.

—Pat Burns, when coaching the NHL's New Jersey Devils, after referees negated a line change that led to Tampa Bay's winning goal in the Stanley Cup playoffs

Oh, don't worry, Harold. I'm as embarrassed about it as you are.

—Roger Neilson, after tight-fisted owner Harold Ballard once asked him to not reveal his salary after signing on to coach the Toronto Maple Leafs

You're so fat you can sit around a table all by yourself.
Is that your real hair or is there a cat sitting on your head?
You could use a bookmark to find all your chins.
You're such an egotist you probably have a mirror on the bathroom ceiling so you can watch yourself gargle.

—*Calgary Herald* columnist Alan Maki, on the top insults Leafs coach Pat Burns and Kings coach Barry Melrose were unloading on one another

Usually you ignore people tapping on the glass but it was persistent, and I think I recognized the knock.

—Toronto Maple Leafs coach Pat Quinn, on his eighty-two-year-old mom, Jean Quinn, trying to catch his attention at a scrimmage

I can make him into the player who swears most on the court.

—Ilie Nastase, on coaching rising Swedish tennis star Henrik Sundstrom

I looked in the mirror one day and I said to my wife, "How many great coaches do you think there are?" She said, "One less than you think."

—Legendary Penn State football coach Joe Paterno

Hopefully, that will get done in time, and if not, shortly thereafter.

—Pittsburgh Steelers coach Bill Cowher, on the prospects of signing 2004 top NFL draft pick Ben Roethlisberger

When you're eating ham and eggs, the chicken that laid the eggs was involved, but the pig that provided the ham was totally committed.

—Former University of Miami football coach Howard Schnellenberger, when asked to explain the difference between involvement and commitment

Bend It Like Neuheisel.

—Jim Armstrong of the *Denver Post*, with news from Hollywood on plans for a movie about the former University of Washington football coach and his NCAA rulebook

BECAUSE IF I DON'T FIND ONE, THEY'LL PUT AN AD IN THE PAPER LOOKING FOR A COACH.

—University of Minnesota football coach Glen Mason, on why he placed a help-wanted ad in the newspaper looking for a kicker

I'm glad it happened in front of the library. I've always emphasized scholarship.

—Former Kansas State football coach Doug Weaver, reminiscing about the time he was hung in effigy on the campus

The first guy who drops a pass, fumbles, or misses a tackle has to go up and change a lightbulb.

—Former Kansas State football coach Jim Dickey, on the lights at the stadium that are mounted on poles and rise 160 feet into the air

Yeah, but not as much.

—Clemson football coach Tommy Bowden, asked if he still loved his father, Bobby, after Florida State (Bobby's team) defeated the Tigers 54–7

It was so muddy, people planted rice at halftime.

—Tony DeMeo, the football coach at Mercyhurst College in Erie, Pennsylvania, after a game played in inclement weather

He said, "Gosh, Dad, that means we're not going to any more bowl games."

—Jim Colletto, Purdue football coach and former assistant at Arizona State and Ohio State, on his eleven-year-old son's reaction after he took the job with the Boilermakers

Working for Lou was pretty good. But the problem was, every morning he'd make the coaches kiss his ring, and he kept the ring in his back pocket.

—Wisconsin football coach Barry Alvarez, roasting former Notre Dame coach Lou Holtz

Jimmy Johnson used to tell us, "Listen, you came to the University of Miami to play football. If you wanted an education, you should have gone to Harvard."

—Michael Irvin of Fox Sports Net's *Best Damn Sports Show Period*

He has a lot of inept ability.

—Hank Bullough, while coaching the Buffalo Bills, on the talents of one of his players

Listen, the man comes in to work at 3:45 A.M. You've got to respect a guy going to work when I'm just getting in.

—Tampa Bay defensive tackle Warren Sapp, on coach Jon Gruden

Tie, Chuck Knox, Seattle, and the flag pole at the Orange Bowl.

—Atlanta columnist Glenn Sheeley on the dullest interview in the NFL

It was a brain transplant. I got a sportswriter's brain so I could be sure I had one that hadn't been used.

—Norm Van Brocklin, former NFL quarterback and coach, talking about his brain surgery

What's the difference between a three-week-old puppy and a sportswriter? In six weeks the puppy stops whining.

—Former NFL coach Mike Ditka

I'm not going to defend myself and, if I did, it would take a long time.

—Former New York Knicks general manager Scotty Stirling, on losing his job

I'm all for it.

—Ex-Tampa Bay Buccaneers head coach John McKay, when asked after another tough loss about his team's execution

I remember a speech our coach, John McKay, was giving us at one point in the season. He was emphasizing that games are lost in the trenches by failing to block and tackle on the front lines. And as he was talking he noticed a lineman asleep in the back. He called his name, woke him up, and asked him, "Where are most games lost?" And the lineman says, "Right here in Tampa, sir."

—Another McKay gem, as told by Steve Spurrier, who was a member of the last winless NFL team, the 1976 Tampa Bay Buccaneers

I heard they used to.

—Indiana Pacers coach Larry Bird, asked if he was aware when he took the job that NBA head coaches speak to the media every day

Heck, that's the first time Caldwell Jones has put his hands up in his whole career.

—Al Bianchi, assistant coach of the Phoenix Suns, after watching Caldwell Jones of the Portland Trail Blazers wave to the crowd during player introductions in Portland

Bill Walton's mom called me the other day. She told me she was so happy that those sportscasters and speech therapists had taught Bill how to speak. But she said they didn't bother to teach him how to stop.

—Legendary UCLA basketball coach John Wooden

CHAPTER 11

PEANUT GALLERY

The sports media has become a monster, covering sports with vigor and in such vivid detail that athletes, coaches, and fans have had to adjust. Most athletes and coaches have come to understand that they will be praised by the media, print or broadcast, when they have success, or when they win championships. But when they lose? Look out. As the Boston Red Sox franchise struggled under the Curse of the Bambino, the public was fully aware of the team's shortcomings in World Series play. When the Red Sox finally exorcized the curse, it was fodder for friends and foes alike.

See you in 2090.

—Headline in the *New York Daily News*, after the Boston Red Sox ended their eighty-six-year World Series drought

The Red Sox and Cubs were in the World Series, and nobody won.

—Doug Robarchek of the *Charlotte (NC) Observer*, describing a dream he had—obviously, before the Red Sox ended the curse

It really is baseball season. After all, Barry Bonds has thrown out the ceremonial first bitch.

—*Sporting News*

Randy Johnson was so dominant in his perfect game against Atlanta, that by the fifth inning [TBS broadcaster] Skip Caray stopped referring to the Braves as "we."

—Bill Scheft of *Sports Illustrated*

A sports journalist is someone who would if he could but he can't, so he tells those who already know how they should.

—British sportswriter Cliff Temple

The basic difference between a sportswriter and a sports-talker, is that one wishes he could write the Great American Novel and the other wishes he could read it.

—Bernie Lincicome of the *Rocky Mountain News*

Self, *Money*, and *True Crime* were already taken.

—*Sports Illustrated*'s Steve Rushin, on the title of the new magazine *Pro*, designed for pro athletes

Security is working great. They're not letting anybody in.

—Jerry Greene of the *Orlando Sentinel*, on the many empty seats at the Athens Olympics

Athens has 4.5 quake, judges give it a 3.9.

—Headline in the *Los Angeles Times* during the Athens Olympics

Hamm refused, but vowed to spend the rest of his life searching for the real winner.

—Randy Turner of the *Winnipeg Free Press*, after U.S. gymnast Paul Hamm was asked to give back his Olympic gold medal, given to him in Athens, after it was discovered he won it because of a judging error

Iraqi Balboa.

—Mike Downey of the *Chicago Tribune*, on Najah Ali, Iraq's one-man Olympic boxing team in Athens for the 2004 games

Here's how dominant the U.S. Women's [Olympic] softball team is. Karl Malone is thinking about joining them so he can win a championship.

—Michael Ventre of msnbc.com

Apparently he was completely lost without a script.

—Michael Ventre, on a reason why the Minnesota Vikings cut former World Wrestling Entertainment champion Brock Lesnar

Baseball would miss Jordan like the Olympics miss Eddie the Eagle.

—Bernie Lincicome of the *Chicago Tribune*, on Michael Jordan's departure from the White Sox

Would you like this week's results, or next week's?

—Iain MacIntyre of the *Vancouver Sun*, after a pro wrestling fan called the sports department for the results of Wrestlemania

Dangerous precedent. Before long, readers will start demanding the *Post* publish future pro wrestling results, too.

—Columnist Randy Youngman, after the *New York Post* started publishing pro wrestling results

It's safe to assume that horse's head won't be ending up in anyone's bed.

—Gregg Drinnan of the *Kamloops (British Columbia) Daily News*, after a Thoroughbred co-owned by Tony Sirico, who plays Paulie Walnuts on *The Sopranos*, had its first career start at Saratoga

Don't be what you're looking at.

—Bill Lankhof of the *Toronto Sun*, spotting a sign on the back of an open trailer hauling racehorses

A racetrack is a place where windows clean people.

—Comedian Danny Thomas

Even after dropping his drawers, he still had on more clothes than Serena Williams.

—Greg Cote of the *Miami Herald*, after Marat Safin mooned the crowd during a French Open match

Gee, those German tax guys took more than the shirt off her back.

—*Cutler Daily Scoop*, after Steffi Graf appeared in a bikini in the *Sports Illustrated* swimsuit issue

Good news is the injuries don't appear to be extensive. Bad news is he spilled the beer.

—Karl Vogel of the *Lincoln (NE) Journal Star*, after golfer John Daly slammed his hand in a car door

Far be it from me to pile it on about Hal Sutton, but do you really want a guy who's been married four times trying to match up people?

—Bill Scheft of *Sports Illustrated*, on the American Ryder Cup captain

Now I feel better. I've only hit one perfect shot in the last twelve years . . . a one-foot putt for par on No. 7 at Pirate's Cove mini golf in Orlando.

—Gary Mason of the *Vancouver Sun*, after Tiger Woods stated in his new book that he's hit only one perfect shot . . . a 3-wood at the British Open

Duval has gone from best player never to have won a major to worst player who has.

—Michael Ventre of msnbc.com, on David Duval's opening-round 83 at the 2003 British Open

In what could be a related story, a paper published in the *Las Vegas Journal of Medicine* predicted Pete Rose would live to be 103.

—Randy Turner of the *Winnipeg Free Press*, on a Yale University study that revealed recreational gamblers sixty-five and older are in better health than their younger counterparts

You're not going to believe this, but a golf ball just landed on my laptop. David Duval must be on the practice range again.

—Mike Bianchi of the *Orlando Sentinel*

Maybe two Young awards should be presented in each league—the Cy for the best pitcher and the Anthony for the worst.

—*Los Angeles Times* columnist Allan Malamud, on hapless Mets pitcher Anthony Young during his streak of twenty-six consecutive losses

It could have been worse. He could have been sentenced to eight weeks at Shea.

—The *Sporting News*, after a spectator who ran onto the field during a New York Mets game was sentenced to eight weeks in jail

He's even-tempered. He comes to the ballpark mad and stays that way.

—Broadcaster Joe Garagiola, on Rick Burleson's aggressiveness

Am I the only one who can't wait for *Baltimore Sun* sportswriter Peter Schmuck to interview Mariners pitcher J. J. Putz?

—Mike Gaynes in the *San Francisco Chronicle*

Philadelphia is the only city in the world where you can experience the thrill of victory and the agony of reading about it the next day.

—Mike Schmidt, when he played third base for the Philadelphia Phillies

Baseball fans, don't miss: "Beverly Hills 90210, Detroit Tigers 0."

—Comic Jenny Church, on Fox's prime-time schedule being structured around the baseball playoffs and World Series

On this date in 1985, pitcher Nolan Ryan recorded his 4,000th strikeout. Four thousand strikeouts. You know what the Detroit Tigers call that? Batting practice.

—Jay Leno

This is the ninth locker room he has been in. Twelve more and he'll be tied with Madonna.

—Comedian Jerry Perisho, on Rickey Henderson joining the L.A. Dodgers

He became the first member of baseball's elusive 30–30–30 club.

—Harry Teinowitz of ESPN Radio, on Jose Canseco being handed a thirty-day jail sentence

The secret? The Brewers weren't there.

—Jerry Greene of the *Orlando Sentinel*, after Milwaukee drew 137,265 fans to its new facility, Miller Park, in just three open houses

This guy is so old that the first time he had athlete's foot, he used Absorbine Sr.

—NBC sportscaster Bob Costas, on aging New York Yankees pitcher Tommy John

Maybe this baseball strike's not such a bad thing.

—NBC's Conan O'Brien, on Michael Bolton's disclosure that he was scheduled to sing the national anthem at the canceled World Series

He used to make subs, now he is one.

—A headline in the *Philadelphia Daily News*, on Phillies replacement catcher Joe Cipolloni, who owns a hoagie and pizza shop in South Philly

Essential question as baseball exhibition season approaches: Can bad pitching beat bad hitting?

—John Eisenberg of the *Baltimore Sun*

Baseball fever—catch it and you're the new shortstop.

—Jay Leno, on Major League Baseball's new slogan

Crowd? This isn't a crowd. It's a focus group.

—New York Mets broadcaster Fran Healy, on the attendance at a game in Montreal

When David Wells testified in court that defendant Rocco Gazioso was "foul-mouthed and insulting," was he considered to be an expert witness?

—Steve Simmons of the *Toronto Sun*

I mean, not even spell-check will help when Jason Simontacchi starts, Gene Stechschulte relieves, and Jason Isringhausen closes.

—Dave van Dyck of foxsports.com, on the difficulties of being the beat writer covering the St. Louis Cardinals

Brooks sings about "Friends in Low Places," so you can see why the Padres used him in a game against the Cubs.

—Steve Rosenbloom of the *Chicago Tribune*, after country music star Garth Brooks appeared as a pinch-runner for San Diego in an exhibition and was thrown out in a Cubs' double play

Well, I see in the game at Minnesota that Terry Felton has relieved himself on the mound in the second inning.

—Kansas City Royals broadcaster Fred White, when the ticker tape from out-of-town games mistakenly showed the same starter and reliever for the Minnesota Twins

I heard the pitching staff was in favor of it, because the 9–0 score would lower the team ERA.

—Baltimore Orioles broadcaster Joe Angel, on the speculation that the Yankees wanted the Tampa Bay Devil Rays to forfeit a game because they arrived late in New York

Weird, isn't it? Something in Arizona getting unretired.

—The *Sporting News*, after the Phoenix Coyotes took Bobby Hull's old No. 9 jersey out of retirement (from the franchise's days as the Winnipeg Jets) so that Brett Hull could wear it in tribute to his dad

Imagine how much higher his average would be if he could bat against himself.

—Dan Daly of the *Washington Times*, on ineffective Colorado Rockies pitcher Mike Hampton batting a gaudy .355

A Gallup Poll indicates half the nation's sports fans don't care if the NHL doesn't play again, and the other half said, "What? It hasn't started yet?"

—Jerry Greene of the *Orlando Sentinel*, on the 2004–05 NHL lockout

If the NHL really wanted to boost TV ratings in the U.S., it would skip the game and go right to the action on 17th Avenue in Calgary.

—Cam Hutchinson of the *Saskatoon StarPhoenix*, on all-female Flames fans who turned postgame celebrations into a "Girls Gone Wild" exhibition during the 2004 Stanley Cup playoffs

So this is how the Avalanche dynasty ends, not with a thump but a snivel. Losing three in a row to a bunch of third-rate prairie mutts, skating like pizza delivery lumps on ice, reaching deep not for the ultimate pursuit but for the ultimate shame, only to find Detroit snuggled against it.

—Bernie Lincicome of the *Rocky Mountain News*, after Colorado lost to the Minnesota Wild in the 2003 NHL playoffs

Murphy will undergo an MRI today to see if he still exists.

—Bernie Miklasz of the *St. Louis Post-Dispatch*, on the St. Louis Blues' Joe Murphy, mired in a long scoring slump

News flash. Six of Canada's edition postage stamps honor former hockey stars [Ray Bourque, Mike Bossy, Bill Durnan, Frank Mahovlich, Stan Mikita, and Serge Savard]. Postal officials, however, nixed plans for a Tie Domi stamp. Turns out it was too tough to lick.

—Dwight Perry in the *Seattle Times*

With the way penalties are being called this season, I'm surprised Mats didn't get two minutes for tripping.

—Hockey commentator Harry Neale, after Dallas Stars captain Derian Hatcher stumbled over a carpet at center ice as Maple Leafs captain Mats Sundin looked on

An investigation is going on. If found guilty, it's a felony punishable by cremation.

—Scott Ostler of the *San Francisco Chronicle*, after hearing reports that dead people voted for the 49ers in their stadium election

The NFL's second-most prominent position is quarterback, right behind hands against the wall and feet spread.

—Rick Morrissey of the *Chicago Tribune*

My broadcast partners are Joe Thiesmann and Dick Vitale, so I am unaccustomed to public speaking.

—ESPN commentator Mike Patrick

One of my uncles was a classic paranoid who couldn't sit through a football game. He thought the guys in the huddle were talking about him.

—Sportswriter Franz Lidz

It's like finding out your mother-in-law has a twin sister.

—New York Giants radio color commentator Dick Lynch, on the Green Bay Packers acquiring receiver John Jefferson to go with their other star receiver, James Lofton

As I recall, Hef's mag figures it'll be the Ravens and Bucs meeting in the Super Bowl, with Baltimore prevailing by a score of 36–24–36.

—Columnist Scott Feschuk, on studying the NFL predictions in *Playboy*

Can't wait. I get goose eggs just thinking about it.

—Randy Youngman of the *Orange County Register*, on the Ravens–Giants Super Bowl, expected to be dominated by defenses

It's a good thing the Ravens and Giants have two weeks to prepare for the Super Bowl. Both teams need time to work on their prevent offense.

—Janice Hough in the *San Francisco Chronicle*

CONSIDERING THEY'VE WON TWENTY OF SIXTY-SIX GAMES, MAYBE THEY SHOULD PIPE IN A LAUGH TRACK.

—Tony Kornheiser of the *Washington Post*, on the New York Jets enhancing their crowd noise

Bye is a four-point favorite.

—Tony Kornheiser, on the 0–7 Washington Redskins having a bye on the weekend

His major is journalism, but because of his 100 touchdown passes, pro scouts may not hold that against him.

—Blackie Sherrod of the *Dallas Morning News*, on Marshall quarterback Chad Pennington

Dick Cheney now is saying that if John Kerry is elected, the country's borders will be protected by the Miami Dolphins' offensive line.

—Mike Bianchi of the *Orlando Sentinel*, using a Republican scare tactic to throw a political football

If you play for the Lions, do you really need a ring finger?

—Mike Bianchi, after Detroit receiver Charles Rogers dislocated his left ring finger during practice

You know it's a strange world, when reporters get more access to the war than they do to NFL teams.

—Bill Reynolds of the *Providence Journal*

Second thought: Vanover tells the team there is no need to pick him up at the airport. He'll find his own transportation.

—Chris Dufresne of the *Los Angeles Times*, after the San Diego Chargers signed kick returner Tamarick Vanover, who spent two months in jail for a stolen-car case

The West Nile offense.

—Paul Daugherty of the *Cincinnati Enquirer*, on the Bengals' attack, which is the opposite of the West Coast offense

The count on the play: two balls, one strike.

—Mike DiGiovanna of the *Los Angeles Times*, after UCLA twin brothers Dave and Mat Ball reached Washington Huskies quarterback Cody Pickett simultaneously, each getting credit for half a sack during a 46–16 rout of Washington

Four out of five dentists still prefer Oklahoma.

—Reggie Hayes of the *Fort Wayne (IN) News-Sentinel*, not impressed that the longest college football winning streak belonged to Colgate

If you build it, they will go.

—Steve Rosenbloom of the *Chicago Tribune*, after a man who graduated from a Michigan high school sixty years ago contributed $20,000 to build bathrooms on the visitors' side of the football field

The Knicks recently retired Patrick Ewing's jersey. In keeping with tradition, it will disappear in the fourth quarter.

—Steve Rosenbloom

Iverson goes by the nickname "The Answer," so the question must be: "Will the defendant please rise?"

—Steve Rosenbloom, after Philadelphia 76ers guard Allen Iverson was charged with drug and firearm possession

Don't pay too much attention to Mike Price's $20 million wrongful termination suit against Alabama. Word is he'll settle out of court for $100 in ones.

—Jeff Schultz of the *Atlanta Journal-Constitution*, on a former University of Alabama football coach who was fired after an evening out with some strippers

TV networks have it written into their contracts that they get walk-off interviews from players and coaches at halftime of basketball and football games. Just wondering if the NBA has a similar deal with Court TV.

—Jeff Schultz

She's a better rebounder than Ben Wallace.

—Jim Armstrong of the *Denver Post*, on Jennifer Lopez saying "I do" for the third time, less than half a year after her breakup with Ben Affleck

Do NBA players think that Dennis Rodman's latest suspension—for deliberately hitting Milwaukee's Joe Wolf in the groin—will teach him a lesson? Well, let's just say they're keeping their legs crossed.

—Bob Lacey of the *Half Moon Bay (CA) Review*

It's got nothing to do with air, kid. That's just what it feels like playing for the Nuggets.

—The *Sporting News*, after NBA rookie Carmelo Anthony compared playing in Denver's mile-high altitude to getting punched in the chest

The Lakers were told that Hefner would be bringing "ten or eleven" of his friends. No indication which month or months were left behind.

—T. J. Simers of the *Los Angeles Times*, after Hugh Hefner of *Playboy* was a guest of Lakers owner Jerry Buss at a playoff game against Houston

Smurfing the Nets.

—Headline in the *Los Angeles Times*, after Shaquille O'Neal hooped forty points for the Los Angeles Lakers against New Jersey in the NBA final

There's a word for a book like that: "Autobiography."

—Greg Cote of the *Miami Herald*, after a new book named Shaquille O'Neal the best basketball player of all time

It's hard to say which city has more to celebrate.

—Steve Abney in the *San Francisco Chronicle*, on the Grizzlies' departure from Vancouver to Memphis

The Golden Blades? What about "Tonya and the Blunt Objects" or "The Rolling Bones"? We wonder if the Blades' song list includes "Cold as Ice" or "Hit Me with Your Best Shot." And when does Tonya's *Greatest Hits* CD come out?

—Tom FitzGerald of the *San Francisco Chronicle*, on Tonya Harding making her public singing debut with her band, the Golden Blades, at a benefit concert in Portland

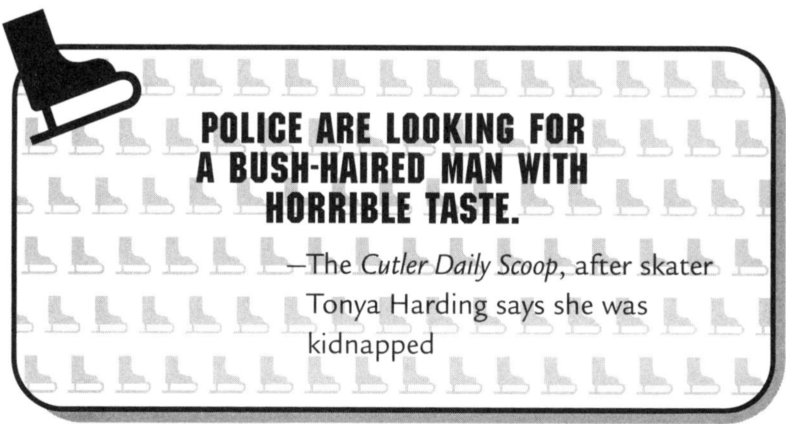

POLICE ARE LOOKING FOR A BUSH-HAIRED MAN WITH HORRIBLE TASTE.

—The *Cutler Daily Scoop*, after skater Tonya Harding says she was kidnapped

The best thing about sailing on TV? No slow-motion replays.

—Syndicated columnist Norman Chad

It wasn't lost on some scribes that Mark Martin's Viagra car was the first to break down at the Daytona 500. Of course, the mechanical problems were complicated when the pit crew lifted the hood and couldn't get it back down again.

—Mike Bianchi of the *Orlando Sentinel*

How many fighters does it take to change a light bulb? None. The promoter will fix it.

—Mike Bianchi

You've got your health, you've got your money, you've even got most of your ear.

—Jim Armstrong of the *Denver Post*, suggesting to Evander Holyfield three good reasons to hang up his boxing gloves

I'd go fifteen more rounds with Holmes if I thought it would get Cosell off football broadcasts.

—Tex Cobb, whose loss to Larry Holmes prompted Howard Cosell to quit boxing telecasts

Retired NBA star Charles Barkley, up $300,000 early in the evening at the Aladdin on Sunday night. Don't you hate to read partial scores in the newspaper?

—*Las Vegas Journal-Review*

Why do the movies always portray reporters, and especially sportswriters, as unkempt, uncaring, uncouth louts who only care about getting sensationalist headlines and free food? It's a bum rap. I'm not uncaring.

—Jerry Greene of the *Orlando Sentinel*

Sould we be worried that his first two recruits are "Lowe" and "Life"?

—Carol Wigg, in Tom FitzGerald's syndicated column, after newly hired UMass basketball coach Travis Ford signed guards James Life and Chris Lowe

The Toronto Blue Jays on Monday replaced a pitcher named Bush (Dave) with a reliever named League (Brandon).

—Karl Vogel of the *Lincoln (NE) Journal-Star*

CHAPTER 12

PUN NETWORK

What's in a phrase? Words. What's in a word? Letters, obviously . . . thanks, smarty pants. But changing just one letter can make all the difference and completely alter the meaning. The final product can be—excuse us here—something that tickles your punny bone. Get ready to groan some more . . .

Boy, the shirt has really hit the fan this time.

—Steve Hornbostel in the *San Francisco Chronicle*, after a spectator at a Florida Marlins game decided to sue because he got hit in the eye by a T-shirt that was launched with an air cannon by the team's mascot

[That's] why he was the sack king.

—Jeff Gordon of the *St. Louis Post-Dispatch*, after Hall of Fame linebacker Lawrence Taylor told CBS's *60 Minutes* that, on the eve of a game, he would hire hookers to visit the hotel rooms of opposing running backs

All good things must come to a mend.

—Bill Lankhof of the *Toronto Sun*, after English Olympic women triathletes discovered that their swimsuits, when wet, were a bit too revealing

Do you know that every athlete that you have seen on your television screen has been tested for drugs? Every single one. Or, as NBC calls it, "Must Pee TV."

—Jay Leno, on the Atlanta Olympics

Guess he heard that was the best place to find an in-turn.

—Randy Turner of the *Winnipeg Free Press*, on former president Bill Clinton going to a curling club during a visit

Till meth do they part.

—Gavin McDougald of couchmaster.ca, on golfer John Daly's wife facing methamphetamine and other charges in Mississippi

Last year was pretty amazing. I could have been studying for finals and midterms [at Stanford], but I got my Masters instead.

—Tiger Woods at the ESPY Awards

It's obvious that the recent slump for Tiger is a case of grin and bear it.

—Associated Press golf writer Doug Ferguson on Woods, who was chased by a bear while fishing in Alaska

I really haven't let it sink in.

—Aaron Gieseke to the *Rochester Democrat and Chronicle*, after his third hole in one in three months

When Craig Stadler teamed at the AT&T with rocker Glenn Frey, I'm surprised he didn't do better. He started each round with an Eagle.

—Bob Lacey, *Half Moon Bay (CA) Review*

Talk about a dead giveaway.

—Bob Lacey, after the minor league Hagerstown (Maryland) Suns and a funeral home offered a free funeral service worth $4,000 to the fan who came up with the most creative send-off plan

So that makes him a restricted free agent?

—Scott Ostler of the *San Francisco Chronicle*, on former baseball slugger Jose Canseco facing two years of house arrest after his thirty-day jail sentence for assault

The player is reported to be both disappointed and itching to play.

—David Thomas of the *Fort Worth Star-Telegram*, after Taiwan lost a player to chicken pox at the Little League World Series

Herndon seems to be bothered by insects at the plate. I don't know what species it is. Maybe it's an infield fly.

—San Francisco Giants announcer Hank Greenwald

I was afraid they'd call me on the infield fly rule.

—Randy Myers while pitching for the New York Mets, after he discovered the zipper on his uniform pants was broken

Montreal Expo starting pitcher Ugueth Urbina's middle name is Urtain. That makes him the only player in major-league history with the initials U.U.U. U the man.

—Steve Springer of the *Los Angeles Times*

How was the Spiders' attendance that year? I'll bet they couldn't draw flies.

—Tom FitzGerald of the *San Francisco Chronicle*, on the 1899 Cleveland Spiders, whose 20–134 record made even the 2003 Detroit Tigers look good (Tigers finished 43–119)

It was announced in the press box as a "ground-pool double."

—Tom FitzGerald, after Arizona's Matt Williams bounced a ball off the warning track and into the swimming pool beyond the right-center field fence at Bank One Ballpark

Foul play is suspected.

—Jim Bainridge of the *Colorado Springs Gazette*, after hearing the average life of a baseball used in a game is six pitches

You can now rest assured that the Mariners have absolutely no plans this season to hold a "fire sale."

—Seattle Mariners broadcaster Dave Niehaus, after the M's bus went up in smoke but fortunately no members of the team were hurt

If the Mariners interview Dusty Baker as the thirteenth managerial candidate, wouldn't that be a—drum roll—Baker's dozen?

—Roy Neese of the *Anchorage Daily News*

Well, they did have a Bob Uecker day off for me once in Philly.

—Ex-major-leaguer Bob Uecker, asked if they ever had a day for him as a player

HOW ABOUT THAT DEAD BODY ON LARRY WALKER'S PROPERTY? USUALLY THE STIFFS ARE PITCHING FOR THE ROCKIES.

—Janice Hough in the *San Francisco Chronicle*

Sorry, but I still can't figure out the right joke about Jeff Kent hitting for the cycle.

—Steve Rosenbloom of the *Chicago Tribune*, after major leaguer Jeff Kent was injured following a motorbike accident

Rough Riders draft a real stiff.

—Headline in an Ottawa newspaper, after the Canadian Football League's Ottawa Rough Riders selected a football player who died in a car accident

The agents' feeling is: The gross is always greener.

—ESPN's Dick Schaap, who suggested NFL free agents from winning teams might be better off re-signing with those teams than taking offers for more money elsewhere

Well, we do have a draw play here.

—Pat McInally, Cincinnati Bengals punter, when asked if the art history courses he took at Harvard had helped him in the NFL

Our people think getting him with our second pick in the second round was highway robbery and that he could be the steal of the draft.

—St. Louis Rams publicist Rick Smith, on draft choice Jesse James

Somebody threw "Rice" at the wedding.

—John Galvin in the *San Francisco Chronicle*, hearing the Steve Young wedding got out of hand

I'm thrilled about this. I'm glowing right now.

—Sammy Lilly, out-of-work NFL cornerback who interviewed for a job at a nuclear power plant in Georgia, after getting a call to play for the Rams

Fiedler on the goof.

—Headline in the *Philadelphia Daily News*, after Miami Dolphins quarterback Jay Fiedler threw a late interception to seal the Philadelphia Eagles' 34–27 victory

Whom does Arizona Cardinals Cornerback Ty Howard love the most? His son Ty, his son Tyrell, or his daughter Tyler? The answer is clear . . . It's a three-way tie.

—Steve Rushin of *Sports Illustrated*

Oh, so that's why they're called cell phones!

—Comedy writer Jerry Perisho, after former Los Angeles Rams defensive back Darryl Henley allegedly used a portable phone for illegal activities while he was in jail

When the team switches from one formation to another before the snap, it will be called the graveyard shift. And we will have an entirely new meaning of the term "coffin-corner kick."

—Scott Ostler of the *San Francisco Chronicle*, on the University of Arkansas at Pine Bluff's plans to build a football stadium on a cemetery site

Nice combination there: Earthwind and Fire.

—Tom FitzGerald of the *San Francisco Chronicle*, on New England Patriots cornerback Earthwind Moreland, who played a couple of seasons with the Rhein Fire of NFL Europe

It was so cold at the Dolphins–Patriots game that when Miami guard Jamie Nails and New England linebacker Ted Johnson knocked heads, Nails' helmet split straight in half. See, amazing things can happen when people put their heads together.

—Tom FitzGerald

A blown fuse that caused an eleven-minute delay in an AFC title game was located near the top of a telephone pole across a highway from Foxboro Stadium. The Massachussets Electric lineman who made the repair? Walter Power.

—Tom FitzGerald

Poor guy must have thought it was an exhibition match.

—Tom FitzGerald, after Japanese sumo wrestler Asanokiri lost a match when his loincloth fell off during a bout, exposing his private parts on national television

He was the best man in our fight, too.

—Boxer Jake LaMotta, at his sixth marriage, on best man Sugar Ray Robinson

If Tyson bites off Lewis' ear in L.A., they'll just quickly reattach it. No big deal. Why do you think they call it the Staples Center?

—Comedian Jerry Perisho

If Evander Holyfield and Mike Tyson fight again, Holyfield will wear on his robe "He Ate Me."

—*San Francisco Chronicle* columnist Scott Ostler, on the "He Hate Me" namebar on XFL player Rod Smart's jersey that could spread to other sports, like boxing

Lennox Lewis is demanding a bonus clause to fight Mike Tyson . . . more money if Tyson fouls . . . so this could be history's first pay-per-chew fight.

—Scott Ostler

Being a good Christian, Holyfield is willing to turn the other ear.

—The *Cutler Daily Scoop*, after Holyfield said he'd forgiven Mike Tyson and would fight him again

When it's all finished and I write a book, if I do, the title will be, *The Only Thing Square Was the Ring.*

—Fight manager Bob Biron

Return to sender!

—What the crowd screamed after Tony Thornton, a U.S. postal worker, delivered a left hook to win the vacant U.S. Boxing Association super middleweight title. The thirty-five-year-old Punching Postman stopped Daren Zenner in the second round.

The problem against the Czechs was that we ran into a hot bartender.

—An unidentified American Olympic hockey player, amid rumors that team members had partied all night prior to the 4–1 loss to the Czech Republic at the Winter Olympics in Nagano

Does that make him a nyetminder?

—Randy Turner of the *Winnipeg Free Press*, on Russian goalie Nikolai Khabibulin turning down a chance to play for Russia in the World Cup of Hockey

A rat trick.

—Florida Panthers goalie John Vanbiesbrouck, after teammate Scott Mellanby killed a rat in the dressing room, and then went out and scored two goals

Sharks coach Darryl Sutter and five of his brothers played in the NHL, but the oldest brother didn't. Gary is a highway commissioner in Canada. I guess he just had to pave the way.

—Ed Rush in the *San Francisco Chronicle*

As an ice-facility chain, we're only as strong as our weakest rink.

—New York Rangers forward Luc Robitaille, on owning a piece of a firm that runs a chain of ice rinks around the country

It would have been a short strike.

—Cam Hutchinson of the *Saskatoon StarPhoenix*, on jockeys threatening to boycott the Kentucky Derby if they weren't allowed to wear advertising on their uniforms

In real estate, I believe they call this a joint venture.

—Cam Hutchinson, on reports that Canadian snowboarder Ross Rebagliati, who nearly lost his 1998 Olympic gold medal after testing positive for marijuana, is being sued by a former girlfriend for her share of a house they purchased together

Which just goes to show you that even in death, some people need to get a life.

—Bill Maher of *Politically Incorrect*, on a company in Germany making coffins in the colors of soccer teams for fans who want to stay true to their teams even after the "final whistle"

If you want to get technical about it, the powerful German entry at this year's Women's World Cup is called the *Die Deutsche Frauen-Nationalmannschaft Weltmeisterschafters*. Headline writers suddenly sense what U.S. soccer pundits have known all along: this team spells trouble.

—Dwight Perry of the *Seattle Times*

Alves has left the building.

—Damon Andrews of KTLA-TV in Los Angeles, after U.S. Open chair umpire Mariana Alves was let go after her wrong overrule in Serena Williams' quarterfinal loss to Jennifer Capriati

A Wimbledon security guard caught three Australian men urinating on center court hours before this year's men's singles final . . . thus giving a whole new meaning to the term "tennis whiz."

—Dwight Perry

Possible punishments include, fittingly enough, a lot of parallel bars.

—Dwight Perry, on Richard Bortkevich, the son of Olympic gymnastics legend Olga Korbut, pleading guilty to counterfeiting charges

It's so much hot Air.

—Ken Rosenthal of the *Baltimore Sun*, on Michael Jordan leading the push to decertify the NBA Players Association

When you have that type of behavior, you've got to weed it out.

—University of Missouri basketball coach Quinn Snyder, after kicking a player off the team for possessing marijuana

Nolan Richardson III resigns as Tennessee State basketball coach after bringing in a .38 handgun to the gym following a dispute with an assistant. Tough spot for Tennessee State. They hate to lose a coach of that caliber.

—Scott Ostler of the *San Francisco Chronicle*

Considering the Nancy Kerrigan incident and now the hubcap tossing at her boyfriend, there's no arguing that Tonya Harding should get full honors for being history's first "dis-figure skater."

—Leigh Hill in the *San Francisco Chronicle*

So if Dirk Nowitzki and Michael Finley play anyway, would you consider them "Cuban" defectors?

—Tim Kawakami of the *San Jose Mercury News*, on threats by Dallas Mavericks owner Mark Cuban to keep his players out of the world basketball championships

Meadowlark Felon.

—Bill Scheft of *Sports Illustrated*, with a nickname suggestion before Harlem Globetrotter Clyde Austin was convicted on fraud charges

I'm all shook up.

—Jayson Stark of the *Philadelphia Inquirer*, who asked Elvis impersonator Ted Prior of Absecon, New Jersey, for his reaction after Cincinnati Reds owner Marge Schott decided that an Elvis Presley shrine should be removed from radio announcer Marty Brennaman's broadcast booth

End of an error.

—Headline in the *New York Post*, after the New York Mets traded Roberto Alomar to the Chicago White Sox

So long to the end of an error.

—David Casstevens of the *Arizona Republic*, on the firing of Arizona Cardinals coach Buddy Ryan

A Utah Jazz usher has hit Dennis Rodman with a lawsuit for allegedly pinching her on the butt. He knew this was coming. Immediately after it happened, she threatened to sue the panties off him.

—Comedy writer Alan Ray

Rick Majerus turned down the Golden State Warriors once he learned the team was over the calorie cap.

—Shaun Powell of *The Sporting News*

Paul Allen fears Pippen eventually will seek joint ownership.

—Sheldon Spencer of espn.com, on why Scottie Pippen, seeking a minority share of the marijuana-laced Portland Trail Blazers, can't get the owner to return his calls

Houston Rockets forward Scottie Pippen was arrested on suspicion of drunk driving a few hours after a loss to Dallas. His mistake was to tell the officers that he just had a "triple-double."

—Comedian Jerry Perisho

You wonder why parents do that to a kid. But he points out there's no quit in sophomore Sur Render.

—Gunnison (Colorado) High School athletic director Larry Mims, on the team's scrappy five-foot-six point guard with an unfortunate name

It's a little-known fact that, since being cited for urinating in public, pitcher Kerry Wood has been listed by the Chicago Cubs as a reliever.

—Baseball enthusiast Sean Callahan

It figures that Sammy is asking for a lighter sentence.

—Scott Ostler of the *San Francisco Chronicle*, on Sammy Sosa appealing his eight-game suspension for having a corked bat

That's what you call "skull-duggery."

—The Associated Press, after popular South Korean pro baseball coach Kim Sung-Han faced a threatened lawsuit after he rapped the helmeted head of a player with a baseball bat during training

CHAPTER 13

YOGI-ISMS

What is a collection of sports quotes without even a mention of the yeti of yakking, Yogi Berra? The funniest part is that Yogi-isms aren't limited to the former Yankees catcher and manager. Many others are quite capable of saying things that boggle the mind. In honor of some of Yogi's best lines—such as, "When you get to a fork in the road, take it"—we present a tribute to the confused mind, with the following head-scratchers worthy of the catcher himself.

Strangely, in slow-motion replay, the ball seems to hang in the air for even longer.

—Yogi Berra

I have just two weapons. My legs, my arms and my brains.

—Atlanta Falcons quarterback Michael Vick

All I'm asking for is what I want.

—Major league baseball all-time stolen base leader Rickey Henderson

Athlete's urine test comes back negative for urine.

—Headline from SportsPickle.com

No comment.

—Michael Jordan, after being asked for his response to making the NBA's All-Interview Team

I didn't even know Elvis was from Memphis. I thought he was from Tennessee.

—Memphis Grizzlies draft pick Drew Gooden, on whether he planned to visit Graceland

He's like that famous painter Liberace.

—Arizona Wildcats basketball player Rick Anderson, showing off his college education in describing teammate Luke Walton

We'd hand them a caramel candy, and if they took the wrapper off before they ate it, they'd get a basketball scholarship. If they ate the caramel with the paper still on it, we'd give them a football scholarship.

—Frank Layden, former Utah Jazz coach, on a test he used to administer to recruits when he coached at Niagara

You don't want me. Pat Riley spends more on a haircut than I do on a sports jacket.

—Frank Layden, to a newspaper fashion editor who had called for an interview

John was born talking. He slapped the doctor.

—Bill Fitch, Houston Rockets coach, talking about extroverted guard John Lucas

No, I wash giraffe ears.

—Artis Gilmore, Chicago Bulls seven-foot-two center, when asked by a fan if he played basketball

It's caught out in center field by the center fielder.

—Broadcaster Ralph Kiner, having difficulty identifying replacement players during a Mets–Indians exhibition game

Closed.

—Yogi Berra, while accepting an honorary degree from Roger Williams University, when asked how he liked school

I'd be the laughingstock of baseball if I changed the best left-hander in the game to an outfielder.

—Ed Barrow, Boston Red Sox manager, on Babe Ruth, in 1918

They're writing a movie about me. It's called the *Summer of Four-to-Three*.

—Andy Van Slyke, Pittsburgh Pirates outfielder, while in the throes of a slump

My wife, so I can see how wonderful it is to live with myself.

—Andy Van Slyke, when asked if there was anyone else in the world he would trade places with for a day

There is one word in America that says it all, and that word is, "You never know."

—Former big-league baseball pitcher Joaquin Andujar

That's why I don't talk. Because I talk too much.

— Joaquin Andujar

How's the donor doing?

—Asked by a reporter at the news conference following Mickey Mantle's liver transplant, the doctor explained that the donor had also given his corneas, lungs, kidney, and heart

Are you a natural left-hander?

—Former major-league pitcher Jim Abbott, who was born with one arm, when asked about his days with Team USA

IS THAT THE BEST GAME YOU EVER PITCHED?

—A media member to Yankees hurler Don Larsen, after his perfect game in the World Series

Were you born that way?

—Question posed to Antonio Alfonseca, who has six fingers on each hand, when he signed with the Chicago Cubs

My family was very poor . . . It was embarrassing . . . When I went bowling, I also had to rent socks.

—Yogi Berra, about his rough upbringing

Never answer an anonymous letter.

—Yogi Berra

So I'm ugly. I never saw anyone hit with his face.

—Yogi Berra

If you slid into bases headfirst for twenty years, you'd be ugly, too.

—Pete Rose

Me.

—Pete Rose, as Reds manager, when asked which baseball player in history he'd most like to be

It's permanent, for now.

—Cincinnati Red Roberto Kelly, announcing his new name would be Bobby

As I remember, the bases were loaded.

—Philadelphia Phillies center fielder Garry Maddox, on his first major-league grand slam

They should have had the bases loaded, because every time I pitched for them, that's what happened.

—Roger Craig, on throwing out the first ball when the New York Mets celebrated their twenty-fifth anniversary

Me and George and Billy are two of a kind.

—Ex-major-leaguer Mickey Rivers, on his relationship with George Steinbrenner and Billy Martin

The game was closer than the score indicated.

—Baseball player Dizzy Dean, after a 1–0 game

Sometimes they write what I say and not what I mean.

—Former Los Angeles Dodgers outfielder Pedro Guerrero, on sportswriters

Sure. I'm proud to be an American.

—Cincinnati Reds pitcher Steve Foster, asked by a Canadian customs agent if he had anything to declare

It's a partial sellout.

—Atlanta Braves broadcaster Skip Caray, trying not to say the game has only drawn 6,000 fans

Haven't they suffered enough?

—Beano Cook, publicist for CBS Sports, after Bowie Kuhn gave the fifty-two former Iran hostages lifetime major league baseball passes

You have a left and a right. The left side controls the right half of your body, and the right side controls the left half. Therefore, left-handers are the only people in their right mind.

—Bill Lee, former Montreal Expos pitcher, on brain hemispheres

Greg Minton is definitely one of the best stoppers in the league because when he enters a game, you can stop thinking about winning.

—A San Francisco fan, on the Giants pitcher

Trying to hit Phil Niekro is like trying to hit Jell-O with chopsticks.

—New York Yankee broadcaster Bobby Murcer

This is truly an international event. We signed an outstanding Mexican pitcher at an Italian restaurant in the middle of Chinatown.

—Los Angeles Dodgers' vice president Al Campanis, on the signing of Fernando Valenzuela

There's a fly to deep center field. Winfield is going back, back. He hits his head against the wall. It's rolling toward second base . . .

—Sportscaster Jerry Coleman, on a play in a New York Yankees game

My daddy can't come to the phone. He is reading the newspaper to find out where he will be pitching next year.

—Angels pitcher Jim Slaton's daughter, on his telephone answering machine

He got him looking for something he wasn't looking for.

—Anaheim Angels color commentator Rex Hudler, after Anaheim pitcher Scot Shields struck out a Kansas City Royals batter looking

It's not that I was wild. It's just that I never threw that many strikes.

—Texas Rangers reliever Mitch Williams, on his control

I was flabbered.

—Former Pittsburgh Pirate Willie Stargell, on a standing ovation at Three Rivers Stadium

I want all the kids to do what I do, to look up to me. I want all the kids to copulate me.

—Chicago Cubs outfielder Andre Dawson, on being a role model

You dead yet?

—Yogi Berra's question to his former New York Yankees battery-mate Whitey Ford, while Ford was battling skin cancer

A lot of good ballgames on tomorrow, but we're going to be right here with the Cubs and the Mets.

—Thom Brennaman, Chicago Cubs broadcaster

Why does everybody stand up and sing "Take Me Out to the Ballgame" when they're already there?

—Former big-league baseball pitcher Larry Anderson

No, my name is Mike.

—Atlanta Braves pitcher Mike Hampton, when an elementary-school youngster asked him if he was rich

That picture was taken out of context.

—New York Mets pitcher Jeff Innis, griping about a bad newspaper photo

Tonight, we're honoring one of the all-time greats in baseball, Stan Musial. He's immoral.

—Johnny Logan, ex-major leaguer, introducing Musial at a banquet

I'll take the two-stroke penalty, but I'll be damned if I'll play it where it lays.

—Elaine Johnson, Canadian golfer, after one of her shots struck a tree, rebounded, and landed in her bra

Through years of experience I have found that air offers less resistance than dirt.

—Jack Nicklaus, on why he tees a golf ball so high

I owe it all to my parents.

—San Francisco Giants rookie pitcher David Aardsma, on ending Hank Aaron's fifty-year reign atop the alphabetical list of big-league players

I OWE A LOT TO MY PARENTS, ESPECIALLY MY MOTHER AND FATHER.

—Pro golfer Greg Norman

I played as much golf as I could in North Dakota but the summer up there is pretty short. It was usually on a Tuesday.

—Pro golfer Mike Morley, talking about golf in his home state

He had the most incredible misdemeanor.

—PGA Tour player Fulton Allem, on the composure shown by Matt Kuchar, low amateur at the Masters

His nerves. His memory. And I can't remember the third thing.

—Lee Trevino, on the three things that go as a golfer ages

Then I was skinnier. I hit it better, I putted better, and I could see better. Other than that, everything is the same.

—PGA Senior Tour player Homero Blancas

Ninety percent of putts that are short don't go in.

—Yogi Berra on golf

I'm broke, and I don't want to get a job. All I own are a Porsche and a suntan.

—Lance Ten Broeck, on why he is playing on the satellite golf tour after losing his PGA card

When a pro hits it left to right, it's called a fade. When an amateur hits it left to right, it's called a slice.

—Pro golfer Peter Jacobsen, on what separates a pro from an amateur

"History wasn't bad," he said. "But World Literature and all that crap? I could care less about what happened, all these fiction stories about what happened in the year 1500 or 1600. Half of 'em aren't even true."

—John Daly, telling *Golf Digest* he wasn't much of a student in college

A little bit . . . he's got this aroma about him.

—British Open champ Ben Curtis, when asked if he was at all intimidated by the presence of Tiger Woods

It's a teaching tool for the coaches, but it's also something we're doing for team bondage.

—Defenseman Curtis Cooper of the Western Hockey League's Prince George (British Columbia) Cougars, to the *Prince George Citizen*, on why the team got together to watch the 2004 World Cup of hockey final

Look at the two idiots. You add up their IQs and it may add up to eleven. And then Lewis said, "Tiger, why don't you jump in there with them and make it an even dozen?"

—Former NHLer Tiger Williams, recalling a conversation he had with referee Bryan Lewis after a Dave Schultz-Kurt Walker fight

Tiger Williams went shopping for a wig the other day and found one he liked. The clerk said that will be $39.99 with tax. Tiger replied: "I don't need any tacks, I'm going to glue it on."

—Rabbi Bregman, speaking on the banquet circuit

A few years ago I couldn't spell author. Now I are one.

—*Hockey Night in Canada* commentator Don Cherry, reflecting on how a person with such rotten grammar could write a book

Better teams win more often than the teams that are not so good.

—Tom Watt, ex-Toronto Maple Leafs coach (his team was not so good)

I gave Gary a hockey puck once, and he spent the rest of the day trying to open it.

—Pat Williams, Orlando Magic general manager, after reports that Gary Bettman, NBA senior vice president, might become commissioner of the NHL

You can sum up this sport in two words: You never know.

—Lou Duva, boxing trainer

Why would anyone expect him to come out smarter? He went to prison for three years, not Princeton.

—Lou Duva, on Mike Tyson hooking up again with promoter Don King

He's a guy who gets up at six o'clock in the morning regardless of what time it is.

—Lou Duva, on the spartan training regimen of heavyweight Andrew Golota

Sure there have been injuries and deaths in boxing—but none of them serious.

—Commentator Alan Minter

He [Julio Cesar Chavez] speaks English, Spanish, and he's bilingual, too.

—Don King, boxing promoter

I never cease to amaze myself. I say this humbly.

—Don King

Because nobody walks out in the middle of my speech.

—Former light-heavyweight boxing champ Archie Moore, on why he prefers to speak at prisons

Fear was absolutely necessary. Without it, I would have been scared to death.

—Floyd Patterson, former heavyweight boxing champion

Not while I'm alive.

—Irving Rudd, boxing publicist, on Howard Cosell's statement that he was his own worst enemy

The trouble with boxing is that it lacks credibility.

—World Wrestling Entertainment owner Vince McMahon

The trouble with boxing is that it lacks credibility.

—World Wrestling Entertainment owner Vince McMahon

That's the dumbest question I ever heard. Actually, you can hit harder with red gloves.

—Unidentified boxer, on being asked if he could hit harder with red gloves or black gloves

No. If you have superstitions, that's bad luck.

—Canadian boxer Eric Lucas, on whether he believes in superstitions

No, I'm a vegetarian.

—Cruiserweight Wali Muhammad, asked if he bit James Salerno during a fight

Even Don King called it a rip-off. He wasn't supposed to quit until the fourth round!

—Jay Leno, on Andrew Golota's surrender after the second round to Mike Tyson

Police said he had an IQ of 100, which of course is only sixty-five Canadian.

—Jay Leno, on the fan who attacked British Columbia Lions cornerback Eric Carter during the CFL playoffs

He can't play unless he plays.

—Wally Buono, head coach of the Canadian Football League's British Columbia Lions, when asked if injured offensive lineman Bobby Singh might suit up against the Calgary Stampeders

If I am not the sexiest man alive, explain why so many women married me.

—Thrice-wed Fox football commentator Terry Bradshaw, on not being chosen for *People* magazine's list of sexiest men

I may be dumb, but I'm not stupid.

—Terry Bradshaw

Usually chips and dip.

—Erik Kramer, Detroit Lions backup quarterback, on what qualities he brought to the "party"

A hotel operator called and said I had been indicted. I panicked and said, "For what?"

—Former All-Pro tight end John Mackey, on how he was informed that he had been elected to the Pro Football Hall of Fame

That windshield factor was really something.

—Former Chicago Bears defensive lineman William "Refrigerator" Perry, on how difficult it was to play in Chicago in the cold of December

We're not attempting to circumcise rules.

—Bill Cowher, Pittsburgh Steelers coach

I don't care what the tape says. I didn't say it.

—Former NFL coach Ray Malavasi

YOU ONLY GET A ONCE-IN-A-LIFETIME OPPORTUNITY SO MANY TIMES.

—Pittsburgh Steelers backup cornerback Ike Taylor, on earning a spot in the starting lineup for an exhibition game

Defensively, I think it's important for us to tackle.

—Karl Mecklenburg, Denver Broncos linebacker

I'm not allowed to comment on lousy officiating.

—Jim Finks, New Orleans Saints general manager, when asked after a loss what he thought of the refs

Nobody in football should be called a genius. A genius is a guy like Norman Einstein.

—ESPN football commentator Joe Theismann

I want to rush for 1,000 or 1,500 yards, whichever comes first.

—New Orleans Saints running back George Rogers, asked if he had set goals for the NFL season

I feel like I'm the best, but you're not going to get me to say that.

—All-time NFL receiving leader Jerry Rice

Hawaii doesn't win many games in the United States.

—Football analyst Lee Corso

He's Mr. Intrigue. He knows the serial number of the Unknown Soldier.

—Sam Rutigliano, ex-Cleveland Browns coach, on Oakland Raiders owner Al Davis

I'm really happy for Coach Cooper and the guys who've been around here for six or seven years, especially our seniors.

—Ohio State quarterback Bob Hoying, after winning a Big Ten title

Most of my clichés aren't original.

—Former NFL coach Chuck Knox

As you all know, there's no "I" in "championship."

—Receiver/defensive back Barry Wagner, before helping the San Jose SaberCats win the Arena Bowl

Even Betty Crocker burns a cake every now and then.

—Texas Tech quarterback Billy Joe Tolliver, after throwing three interceptions in his team's 45–14 loss to Baylor

A sportscaster is a person who can memorize the uniform numbers of fifty players on an NFL team but can't remember which dry cleaner has his shirts.

—NBC's Bob Costas

It would be like putting lipstick on a pig.

—New York sportscaster Fran Healy, on putting a dome over Candlestick Park in San Francisco

To win, I'd run over Joe's mom, too.

—Matt Millen of the Raiders, upon hearing Joe Jacoby of the Redskins say "I'd run over my own mother to win the Super Bowl"

Probably the Beatles' White Album.

—Steve Largent, Seattle Seahawks receiver, talking about the record he would cherish the most when he retired

I taught Jack a lot—how to tie his shoes, how to brush his fangs.

—Ray Mansfield, former Pittsburgh Steelers center, roasting Jack Lambert

Left hand, right hand, it doesn't matter. I'm amphibious.

—Charles Shackleford, of the North Carolina State University basketball team

Any time Detroit scores more than 100 points and holds the other team below 100 points, they almost always win.

—Former NBA coach Doug Collins

We're going to turn this team around 360 degrees.

—NBA guard Jason Kidd

[My] career was sputtering until [I] did a 360 and got headed in the right direction.

—NBA star Tracy McGrady, after signing with the Orlando Magic

Are you any relation to your brother Marv?

—New Jersey Nets guard Leon Wood, introducing himself to the team's TV commentator, Steve Albert

It's almost like we have ESPN.

—Magic Johnson, on how well he and Los Angeles Lakers teammate James Worthy work together on the court

My sister's expecting a baby, and I don't know if I'm going to be an uncle or an aunt.

—Chuck Nevitt, North Carolina State basketball player, explaining to Coach Jim Valvano why he appeared nervous at practice

Tom.

—Tom Nissalke, new coach of the NBA's Houston Rockets, when asked how he pronounced his name

I'll always be No. 1 to myself.

—Former NBA star Moses Malone

You can say so much about so many things so often. But if you do, then you'll be saying nothing about anything all of the time.

—Former Cleveland Cavaliers forward Edgar Jones

Talk doesn't hurt you. Talk is just a figure of speech.

—Charles Oakley, Knicks forward, when New York papers speculated he would be traded

No, but they gave me one, anyway.

—Elden Campbell, L.A. Lakers forward, when asked if he had earned his degree from Clemson

It was nice to be out there long enough to get a feel for the game.

—Charlie Sitton, reserve forward for the Dallas Mavericks, after playing for two seconds in a victory over Portland

What's a province?

—Toronto Raptors forward Tony Massenburg, when asked how many provinces there are in Canada

It's a nice bonus but, you know, I have to pay taxes too.

—Venus Williams, after winning the Grand Slam Cup in tennis

The lead car is absolutely unique, except for the one behind it, which is identical.

—Commentator Murray Walker

It's basically the same, just darker.

—Alan Kulwicki, stock car racer, on racing Saturday nights as opposed to Sunday afternoons

This is really a lovely horse, I once rode her mother.

—Ted Walsh, horse racing commentator

Moses Kiptanui—the nineteen-year-old Kenyan, who turned twenty a few weeks ago . . .

—Commentator David Coleman

Morcelli has four fastest 1500-meter times ever. And all those times are at 1500 meters.

—David Coleman

When Ken sees it, he's going to dump Barbie like a hot potato.

—Gene Nelson, KSFO San Francisco announcer, after the flashy Florence Griffith-Joyner doll made its debut

If history repeats itself, I should think we can expect the same thing again.

—Commentator Terry Venables

There is ski jumping and then there is ski dropping.

—An Italian journalist, speaking of British ski jumper Fast Eddie Edwards

You have to kiss a few toads before you find the right prince.

—Calla Urbanski, U.S. figure skater, after dropping Rocky Marval, her sixth pairs partner

In water like that it's difficult to pick up much ground.

—Tony Johnson, Yale crew coach, on the rough water at the Cincinnati Regatta

Great trade. Who did we get?

—Lenny Dykstra, Philadelphia Phillies outfielder, after hearing the club dealt outfielder Von Hayes to the California Angels

They ought to sound a siren when I pitch, like they do in a tornado.

—Boston pitcher Al Nipper, after Minnesota's Kent Hrbek hit a 477-foot homer off him

I've been traveling so much I haven't had time to grow it.

—Bob Horner, Atlanta Braves third baseman, on why he didn't have a beard anymore

All I said was that the trades were stupid and dumb, and they took that and blew it all out of proportion.

—Ron Davis, Twins pitcher, objecting to a newspaper story in which he was quoted as criticizing Minnesota management for trading away their best players

You don't look so hot, either.

—Yogi Berra, on being told by the mayor's wife that he looked cool, despite the heat

MAN IT WAS TOUGH. THE WIND WAS BLOWING ABOUT 100 DEGREES.

—Mickey Rivers, Texas Rangers DH, complaining about the weather during a game

Tell Len I'm very proud of him. I hope he does better next time.

—Tokie Lockhart, after her grandson Len Barker pitched a perfect game

It couldn't have happened to a greater guy. Well, yes it could. It could have happened to me.

—Los Angeles Dodgers manager Tommy Lasorda, on Jerry Reuss' no-hitter

I've been a huge Sox fan since 1981. It'll be an honor to me to squat in his footsteps.

—Catcher Josh Paul, the Chicago White Sox's No. 2 pick in the Major League Baseball draft, on being a fan of former catcher Carlton Fisk

The average attendance at Cubs games is 48 degrees.

—Chicago Cubs announcer Harry Caray

I was a victim of circumcision.

—Pittsburgh Pirates pitching coach Pete Vukovich, after being ejected from a game for arguing from the dugout

Omar Vizquel sympathizes everything that's good about the Cleveland Indians.

—Indians infielder Jim Thome, accepting an award for a teammate

I had maybe forty to sixty grand a year from Rawlings never to be seen using their stuff.

—Milwaukee Brewers broadcaster and ex-catcher Bob Uecker, on the equipment deals he had during his not-so-stellar playing career

Ever stop to think, and forget to start again?

—Bob Uecker

I'm always suspicious of guys who've got a famous father.

—President George W. Bush, speaking to Arizona Diamondbacks general manager Joe Garagiola Jr. when the World Series champs visited the White House

Bob Dole said, "I sure hope whoever buys them doesn't take them out of Brooklyn."

—Comedian Alex Kaseberg, on the news that the Dodgers are for sale

I was misquoted.

—Charles Barkley, on his autobiography

Since he said it on national TV, it goes down as his lamest denial since he said he had been misquoted in his autobiography.

—Mark Heisler of the *Los Angeles Times* after Charles Barkley of the Phoenix Suns claimed his criticism of club owner Jerry Colangelo had been taken out of context

CHAPTER 14

THE LAST WORD

Any good book needs a strong ending, so some gems have been left for last. So many writers, commentators, observers, fans, athletes, and coaches are quick with the wit, tossing out humorous lines that tickle the funny bone and illuminate issues in the world of sports. Here is a tribute to some of the best in the business—the grande finale, where the best has definitely been saved for last.

The guy who invented the hokey-pokey just died. It was a weird funeral. First, they put his left leg in . . .

—Rae Lorimer

Martha Stewart will attend Yankees camp and try on a uniform to see how she looks in a striped outfit.

—Elliott Harris of the *Chicago Sun-Times*, on George Steinbrenner's next big-name signing

I've been trying to do that for years.

—Tiger Woods, after Michael Ready, eight, hit a shot that almost hit a photographer during Woods' youth clinic in Oklahoma City

I won't be active in the day-to-day operations of the club at all.

—George Steinbrenner, after purchasing the New York Yankees from CBS

So now they are both in New York. Bevis plays for the Mets and Butthead still owns the Yankees.

—Comedian Jerry Perisho, after the New York Mets acquired pitcher P. J. Bevis from Arizona

Q: How many Lakers does it take to change a light bulb?
A: None. They'd rather sit in the dark so they can't see each other.

—Syndicated columnist Norman Chad, on the Los Angeles Lakers

If a coach goes to the Finals four times in five years, I'll kiss his feet on *Fear Factor* . . . with cheese on them.

—Miami Heat center Shaquille O'Neal on the virtues of Phil Jackson, his coach with the Los Angeles Lakers

I'm like toilet paper, toothpaste, and certain amenities . . . I'm proven to be good and useful.

– Shaquille O'Neal on joining the Miami Heat

I'm like the Pythagorean theorem. Not too many people know the answer to my game.

– Shaquille O'Neal

I can't really remember the names of the clubs that we went to.

—Shaquille O'Neal, on whether he had visited the Parthenon during his visit to Greece

In his big scene, he throws a basketball into the ocean. He actually got it on his fifth try.

—Comedy writer Alex Kaseberg, on Shaquille O'Neal appearing on *Baywatch*

The Lakers are looking for at least two starters whom Kobe Bryant is comfortable not getting the ball to.

—Bill Scheft of *Sports Illustrated*, on a package the Lakers were hoping to get in an O'Neal trade

Hiring Magic Johnson as host of a talk show was like drafting Oprah to cover Shaq in the low post.

—Jeff McGregor of the *New York Times*, on the canceled *Magic Hour*

You ever think we'd get to the point when one day kids would be trading basketball cards? "I'll give you two Shaquille O'Neals for an Orgasm."

—Jay Leno, on Dennis Rodman's statement that he wants to legally change his name to Orgasm

Do you think Dennis Rodman really plans to change his name to "Orgasm," or is he just faking it?

—Bob Lacey of the *Half Moon Bay (CA) Review*

Instead of skipping practice, now he'll be missing rehearsal.

—Bob Lacey, after Dennis Rodman signed a contract with World Championship Wrestling

I didn't want to feel the pain of loss. Some people turn to drugs and alcohol. I ended up marrying Dennis Rodman.

—Actress Carmen Electra, on how she coped with the deaths of her mother and sister

I don't know. But I know my hands are tired from stuffing the ballot box.

—Cedric Ceballos of the Los Angeles Lakers, when asked about his chances of being voted a starter in the NBA All-Star Game

Boxing promoter Don King took a ride on a dogsled. It was so cold, he had his hands in his own pockets.

—Chris Myers of Fox Sports News

Today, Tyson received a bill from Don King for $4,999.

—Comedian Alex Kaseberg, on Mike Tyson being down to his last $5,000

Hear about the Tyson computer? Two bytes. No memory.

—Phil Rosenthal of the *Chicago Sun-Times*

Mike said today he's trying to eat less fat as he gets older.

—Jay Leno, on why Tyson won't fight George Foreman

They're both gonna last two weeks.

—Chris Rose of Fox Sports Net, on what John McEnroe's new talk show on CNBC and the U.S. Open tennis championships have in common

The WWE is launching an all-wrestling channel. Twenty-four hours a day of phony conflicts, fake story lines, and deceptive self-promotions. Or, as they call it in Washington, "Decision 2004."

—Comedian Alan Ray

I had my medal on.

—U.S. goalkeeper Briana Scurry, making good on her promise to "run naked through the streets of Athens" if her soccer team won gold in Atlanta. Scurry made the run at 2 A.M., but she told Dave Kindred of *The Sporting News* she wasn't entirely naked

IBM made a big mistake when they laid off half their pawns.

—Comedian Argus Hamilton, on Gary Kasparov's chess win over an IBM supercomputer

You gotta give Alex Rodriguez credit for one thing. He's only been a Yankee for a couple of days, and he's already involved in community service, public service, that kind of thing. Today, what he decided to do was pay a visit to the less fortunate—and so he drove past Shea Stadium.

—David Letterman

I BOUGHT THIS VERY RARE ITEM—A TAX FORM SIGNED BY DARRYL STRAWBERRY. THIS IS THE HOTTEST THING OUT THERE NOW.

—Comedian Billy Crystal, on sports memorabilia

We thought Barry would enjoy seeing lots of strikes.

—Publicist Rachael Vizcarra Banvard, on why the Barry Bonds birthday bash was staged at a bowling alley in Hollywood

Now he can relate to the reporters who have to interview him.

—Bret Lewis of KFWB Radio in Los Angeles on Barry Bonds' root canal surgery

He was brought to Seattle to throw out the first glove.

—Tom Keegan of the *New York Post*, on former Los Angeles detective Mark Fuhrman, whose brother is a friend of pitcher David Wells, being at the Yankees' workout in Seattle

He looks less comfortable donning a glove than anyone since O. J.

—Steve Rushin of *Sports Illustrated,* on Los Angeles Dodgers' outfielder Bobby Bonilla

They asked me if there was anything special they could do for me. I asked if I could have a ball signed by Albert Belle. They said, "Wow, you really are a comedian!"

—Comedian Elaine Boosler, in *Inside Sports* magazine, talking about throwing out the first pitch at a Cleveland Indians game

Talking about Dallas Green's patience is like talking about Dolly Parton's elbows.

—Marty Noble of *Newsday*, on somebody's comment that New York Mets manager Dallas Green has exceptional patience

The first 5,000 fans will receive an autographed police sketch of Dwight Gooden.

—David Letterman, on the New York Mets' season opener

Only the chicken garnered any attention from security personnel.

—Chris Isidore of cnnmoney.com, after New York police detective Patrick Brosnan brought his son some fried chicken and carried his handguns to Yankees and Mets games

Montana 90, Rice 81 in double-overtime.

—A college basketball score that might have caught the eye of San Francisco 49ers fans

First, the bad news: The San Diego Chargers were unfairly harassed by the snowball-throwing New York Giants' fans. Now, the good news: The Mets may have finally found a pitching staff.

—Comedy writer Jerry Perisho

My marriage, the birth of my children, my first day in the big leagues, they all pale in comparison to this.

—Philadelphia Phillies reliever Dave Leiper, after hitting the first batting-practice homer of his eight-year big-league career

Yeah, but I was in the backseat.

—John Salley, former NBA player and Fox Sports Net studio host, when asked if he ever received a police escort in New York City

Back when he was a freshman and really "country," Reeves supposedly told a flight attendant that his ears were bothering him because of the cabin pressure. She suggested that some chewing gum might help, and so Big Country peeled the wrapper off a stick of gum and stuck it in his ear.

—Dan Shaughnessy of the *Boston Globe*, on Oklahoma State center Bryant "Big Country" Reeves

Madonna turned forty-two today [August 2000]. I sent her a dozen long-stemmed basketball players.

—CBS's Craig Kilborn

I like to watch the NBA All-Star Game, or, as I like to refer to it, the Madonna Home Shopping Network.

—David Letterman

I love his intangibles and his loose balls.

—TNT pro basketball analyst Danny Ainge, praising former teammate Dan Majerle on the air

For years, people have been saying that they'd like to play golf like me. Now they can.

—Jack Nicklaus, on his woeful golf game

USA may be the favorite, because they only televise Thursdays and Fridays, and I'm not used to working weekends.

—Slumping golfer David Feherty, on the CBS and USA Networks approaching him about being a commentator

Don Cherry would be proud. I mean, she did take out the Russian.

—Bill Lankhof of the *Toronto Sun*, after Canadian and world champion Perdita Felicien fell in the 100-meter hurdles final at the Olympics in Athens

He had to because they were in the same grade.

—*Hockey Night in Canada* host Ron MacLean, on fellow commentator Don Cherry walking his son to school every day

He's been great at every level he's played at except the NHL, the Olympics, and the world championships.

—Edmonton Oilers general manager Glen Sather, on goalie Tommy Salo, whom the Oilers acquired from the New York Islanders

I went into the corner with him and came out of it with a broken nose and a two-minute penalty. All Gordie got out of it was the puck.

—Eric Nestorenko, recalling his days with the Chicago Blackhawks and his battles with Gordie Howe of the Detroit Red Wings and his elbows

You've got two eyes and one mouth. If you keep two open and one closed, you'll learn a lot.

—Gordie Howe, recalling the advice he gave Wayne Gretzky when he broke into the NHL

That's not true. I've switched to Minneapolis now.

—Ex-Minnesota North Stars goalie Gump Worsley denying an allegation that he did all his training in St. Paul bars

Evidently there's a personality conflict here. For instance, Cujo actually has one.

—Toronto comedian Frenchie McFarlane, on the unease between Detroit Red Wings goalies Dominik Hasek and Curtis Joseph

[They're] the only team whose Zamboni guy has a designated driver.

—Tom Arnold, *Best Damn Sports Show Period* host, on the Tampa Bay Lightning trying to drum up season-ticket business with an offer of free beer during the playoffs

A TV station reportedly asked folks in Tampa Bay if they had watched the Lightning. Seventy percent responded that they hadn't even heard the thunder.

—Janice Hough in the *San Francisco Chronicle*

Lord Stanley, at age 163, is relocating to Florida. Welcome, Stan. A lot of Canadians your age live here.

—Gary Shelton of the *St. Petersburg Times*, on the Tampa Bay Lightning winning the 2004 Stanley Cup

The first player to ask for it can have it.

—Vancouver Canucks general manager Brian Burke, when asked if the Canucks would retire Pavel Bure's number ten after the hold-out star forward was traded to the Florida Panthers

Tobago.

—Sprinter Ato Boldon of Trinidad and Tobago, when asked what his country would give him if he won a gold medal in the Olympics

The sixty-three-year-old president of Rice University, Malcolm Gillis, plans to fight ex-heavyweight champ George Foreman in a charity bout. Obviously, the old man has no business being in a ring. And the same goes for Gillis.

—Greg Cote of the *Miami Herald*

I love exercise. I could watch it all day.

—Former NBA great Bill Russell

It wasn't all bad news. In a joint press release, the club announced it was lowering expectations.

—Chris Dufresne of the *Los Angeles Times*, after the Los Angeles Clippers raised ticket prices following their eleventh consecutive losing season

Until there's a settlement, there'll be no three-pointers. No slam dunks. No alley oops. No fast breaks. For the Los Angeles Clippers, it means business as usual.

—Comedy writer Alan Ray, on NBA owners locking out the players

Happy April Fools' Day. This, of course, is the day we honor people who bet on the Clippers.

—Jay Leno, on L.A.'s other basketball team

We're surprised he didn't ask the Clippers to move to Eagle, Colorado.

—Ted Wyman of the *Winnipeg Sun*, on reports that Kobe Bryant asked the Los Angeles Clippers to play ten to twelve home games a season at the Arrowhead Pond, which is closer to his home, as a condition of signing with them

The Knicks were absolutely right to bring in Latrell Sprewell, because everybody deserves a twenty-second chance.

—Mitch Lawrence of the *New York Daily News*

He's in the top two.

—Larry Bird, when asked if Michael Jordan is the greatest of all time

When you look up and see those championship banners, just think of me.

—Larry Bird, on the message he sent via video as the Boston Celtics saluted Charles Barkley at the FleetCenter

You know what else you can do in four-tenths of a second? Fast forward through your monologue.

—Los Angeles Lakers guard Derek Fisher, to Jay Leno after the buzzer-beating, game-winning shot in the 2004 NBA Western Conference semifinal against the San Antonio Spurs

You know, when Kenny and Charles first came into the league, they didn't speak English, either.

—Commissioner David Stern, responding to comments made by TNT analysts Kenny Smith and Charles Barkley during the NBA draft show that Chinese center Yao Ming's inability to understand English will be a problem for the Houston Rockets, especially at the end of games

These folks are from HBO. We're doing a little segment on *Sex and the City*.

—Detroit Tigers announcer Ernie Harwell, eighty-four, as a camera crew followed him around Comerica Park

Hitting a baseball or a softball is the toughest thing to do in sports. Especially when I'm pitching.

—U.S. softball pitcher Lisa Fernandez, before her mind-boggling twenty-five-strikeout performance against Australia

He once got back to the hotel after a night on the town and he called the front desk and asked for a 7 A.M. wake-up call. The operator said, "You just missed it."

—Los Angeles Dodgers announcer Vin Scully, recalling former big-league infielder Gene Freese

I'm a Republican, my father was a Republican, and his father was a Republican. So someone once asked me, "If your father was a thief and his father was a thief, would that make you a thief?" I said, "That would make me a Democrat."

—Former Los Angeles Dodgers manager Tom Lasorda

That made me think about dying, but it didn't make me think about quitting.

—Honored for his thirty years broadcasting baseball in Milwaukee, Bob Uecker said undergoing heart surgery didn't make him think about retirement

It's the same old problem. When he tried to throw his hat into the ring, it sailed into the seats behind first base.

—Comedian Argus Hamilton, on former big-league second baseman Steve Sax's withdrawal as a candidate for the California Assembly

IT WAS SO HOT IN NEW YORK TODAY, JENNIFER LOPEZ MARRIED TED WILLIAMS.

—David Letterman, with an update on the weather

Of course, when you think about it, aren't all pitches ceremonial at Wrigley these days?

—Phil Rosenthal of the *Chicago Sun-Times* after the Cubs had three ceremonial pitches before a game

He'd give you the shirt off his back. Of course, he'd call a press conference to announce it.

—Pitching great Catfish Hunter, on Reggie Jackson in 1977

On whether he ever tasted one of Jackson's Reggie Bars: "I unwrapped it, and it told me how good it was."

—Catfish Hunter

It's like they say, the guy could hit in his sleep.

—Jim Armstrong of the *Denver Post*, after Major League Baseball credited Hack Wilson with an extra RBI, sixty-nine years after the fact and fifty-one years after his death

She plans to use her free time hitting homers for the Giants.

—Greg Cote of the *Miami Herald*, on sprinter Kelli White getting a two-year ban thanks to the BALCO steroids scandal

Does this mean the Twins will become the Triplets?

—Steve Baker of KVMR-FM in Nevada City, on the possible move of the Minnesota Twins to the Greensboro–High Point–Winston Salem, North Carolina's Triad region

There's no question I'm unpopular, and I felt I needed to get away. So I got in my car and pulled up to a Motel 6. They turned the light off.

—White Sox owner Eddie Reinsdorf, at his charity roast in Chicago

Hey, why not Don Zimmer to succeed Grady Little as Red Sox manager? The Yankees' coach has certainly demonstrated the job's No. 1 requirement—the willingness to head for the mound and take out Pedro.

—Dwight Perry of the *Seattle Times*

I just about shot my age about a week after my eightieth birthday, but I three-putted the hole with the windmill.

—Broadcaster Lon Simmons, who received the Ford C. Frick Award at the Baseball Hall of Fame, on the state of his golf game

The Cleveland Indians traded infielder Stubby Clapp for a player to be named better.

—Bud Geracie, *San Jose Mercury News*

I don't know how much money the folks in Philadelphia spent on dynamite to blow up Veterans Stadium, but I have to believe it would've accomplished the same thing and been cheaper just to let LaTroy Hawkins pitch an inning.

—Steve Rosenbloom of the *Chicago Tribune*

Where's your wife, pal? One of our players is missing.

—Outfielder Jimmy Piersall to a taunting bleacher fan

In this case, it truly was a trade for a player to be named later.

—Atlanta Braves general manager John Schuerholz, on finding out minor-league outfielder Manuel Mateo, acquired by the San Francisco Giants, was actually named Melvin Valdez

A bleacher bum in the right-field stands at Wrigley Field calls an usher over and says, "These guys are bothering me." "Which guys?" the usher asks. The fan points to the Cubs.

—*New York Times*

We're not the problem—and we're definitely not the solution.

—Florida Marlins pitcher Steve Fireovid, on his fellow replacement players

They should have waited for the Clinton Memorial to be built.

—Ron Rapoport of the *Chicago Sun-Times*, after a dozen members of the Ohio State's women's rugby team posed topless in front of the Lincoln Memorial. The captain of the team said they "wanted to do something crazy" to feel more united.

He officially opens the Olympics July 19. In honor of his administration, synchronized lying will be a demonstration sport.

—Comedian Argus Hamilton, on President Bill Clinton's tour of the Olympic facilities in Atlanta

So Tonya Harding is embarking on a career as a recording artist. Let's hope Whitney Houston still has that bodyguard.

—Bob Lacey of the *Half Moon Bay (CA) Review*

Tonya Harding.

—Stanford basketball coach Mike Montgomery, asked if anyone could stop Duke

Lucky for her, Tonya's not the jealous type.

—Jay Leno, after Harding's ex-husband, Jeff Stone [the former Jeff Gillooly], married Tonya's hairdresser

And now this news from the figure skating world: Boston [AP]—Nancy Kerrigan switched from "Why me?" to "I do" on Saturday when she married her agent in a church ceremony closed to fans, reporters, and club-wielding rivals.

—Tom FitzGerald of the *San Francisco Chronicle*

We're delighted that Deion "Prime Time" Sanders will host *The New American Sportsman* outdoors show on ESPN, and we're looking forward to the first episode, "Hooked on Me."

—Tom FitzGerald

Newborns apparently aren't the only things Jackson family members like to dangle in front of large audiences.

—topfive.com, on the Super Bowl halftime show

One informed him that he tied Jeff Graham for the Brian Piccolo award for veterans, given to the player who exemplifies the courage, loyalty, teamwork, dedication, and sense of humor of the late Piccolo. The other informed him he was no longer a Bear.

—Don Pierson of the *Chicago Tribune*, after Chicago Bears defensive back Shaun Gayle got two phone calls from club officials

The NFL means business. The 49ers have been assessed a fifteen-yard penalty for excessive celebration over the departure of Terrell Owens.

—Scott Ostler of the *San Francisco Chronicle*, on NFL commissioner Paul Tagliabue's vow to crack down on end-zone celebrations

Prosecutors showed pictures of O. J. Simpson wearing gloves during a Bengals playoff game. Jurors were stunned with disbelief—the Bengals in the playoffs?

—*Cutler Daily Scoop*

The 49ers got Brandon Whiting for a player to complain later.

—Comedian Alan Ray, on the Terrell Owens trade to Philadelphia

They're doing more with less talent than anyone since Madonna.

—Fox football commentator Marv Levy, on the 2000 Detroit Lions

The New York Giants announced that seventy-five season-ticket holders who threw snowballs during the San Diego game will be banned from attending any more Giants games. I don't think they should be rewarded for that kind of behavior.

—Conan O'Brien

Holdout Seahawks receiver Joey Galloway is playing quarterback in a flag football league in Wheeling, West Virginia. And he still complains he doesn't get the ball enough.

—Syndicated columnist Norman Chad

Area fans are shocked. It's the first time this season he's hit someone who was open.

—Comedy writer Alan Ray after Indianapolis Colts quarterback Jim Harbaugh broke his hand punching Jim Kelly, the former Bills quarterback-turned-sportscaster

When Moon calls an audible, he barks out Roman numerals.

—Syndicated columnist Norman Chad, on forty-year-old quarterback Warren Moon of the Seattle Seahawks

Monday Night Football is on cable? Well, now Nicolette Sheridan won't need a towel.

—Bill Sheft of *Sports Illustrated*

The NFL is thinking about starting Monday night football games an hour earlier next year. Apparently Frank Gifford has been having trouble making his curfew.

—Conan O'Brien

Guess the Bears figure that it ought to cost a lot of money to get to the place the Bears themselves can't get to.

—Steve Rosenbloom of the *Chicago Tribune*, after the Chicago Bears raised ticket prices for its end-zone seats

How many people watched that stupid show, *The Littlest Groom*? It has twelve female little people competing for a little groom. I didn't even know Doug Flutie was dating again.

—Jay Leno

Joe Horn of the New Orleans Saints was fined $30,000 for his little cell phone stunt—$30,000 for making one phone call. And you thought your wireless plan sucked.

—Comedian Alex Kaseberg

Bledsoe's been hit so much the last month, he was made an honorary Liza Minnelli husband.

—Bill Scheft of *Sports Illustrated*, on the pounding absorbed by Buffalo Bills quarterback Drew Bledsoe

The Cowboys are now getting close to having more bad baseball players than the Texas Rangers.

—Bret Lewis of KFWB-LA, after the Dallas Cowboys gave an eight-year contract to quarterback Drew Henson, who, like Quincy Carter and Chad Hutchinson, returned to football after struggling in pro baseball

In kicking terms, that is known as splitting the upright.

—Comedian and broadcaster Jim Barach, after Jacksonville Jaguars punter Chris Hanson accidentally cut himself in the leg with an axe left in the locker room as a motivational tool

Jon Gruden's promise to dance down a Tampa highway in nothing but a jockstrap if his team wins the Super Bowl again this season brings new meaning to the words "Buc naked."

—Bob Molinaro of the *Norfolk Virginian-Pilot*

First, Shockey claimed he was misquoted, then "misinterpreted," and then he apologized. Now he says the remark shouldn't count because he made it during the exhibition season.

—Bill Scheft of *Sports Illustrated*, on New York Giants tight end Jeremy Shockey referring to Cowboys coach Bill Parcells in a magazine article as a "homo"

This is great. It's like they're singing to me every game.

—Winnipeg Blue Bombers import lineman Tom Canada, on hearing the national anthem before Canadian Football League games

It's a retirement community. If it wasn't for mouth-to-mouth resuscitation, there'd be no romance at all in that town.

—Comedy writer Argus Hamilton, on Phoenix as a Super Bowl site

Their pedestrian lights flash "Mosey" and "Don"t Mosey."

—Argus Hamilton, on the pace of life in Phoenix

Fourteen-year-old soccer star Freddy Adu will play for the MLS club DC United, and the league has a right to consider his signing a coup, for one thing, at many hotels, he'll stay free.

—Comedian Alan Ray

There is a word for a person whose life is held hostage by a fourteen-year-old: Parent.

—Greg Cote of the *Miami Herald*, on Freddy Adu signing with DC United, which should save coach Ray Hudson since Adu says he wants Hudson back as coach

The other Trail Blazers expressed disappointment. Not only has he brought embarrassment to the organization, he didn't share.

—Alan Ray, after Portland forward Zach Randolph was charged with driving under the influence after a police officer smelled marijuana in his car

The Supreme Court has ruled that police officers may break into a home twenty seconds after pounding on the front door. There was one stipulation: If it's the home of an NBA player, they'll want to use the full twenty-four seconds.

—Comedian Jerry Perisho

This is like our crowds in Atlanta.

—Toronto Raptors guard Dion Glover, to ten media members gathered around him during his first practice with the team after being waived by the Hawks

Allen Iverson, upon accepting his top rookie honors, credited the guys who took the ball out of bounds.

—Peter Vecsey of the *New York Post*

This ain't like the old days, when you'd hear on the public address, "Will the lady who lost her five kids come and get them? They're beating the Nets."

—New Jersey center Jayson Williams on the Nets' improvement

Could you tell the bachelor's party was last night?

—Detroit Pistons gunner Jerry Stackhouse, after a six-for-twenty-two shooting night on the eve of his wedding

If you were my wife, I'd eat it.

—NBA ref Earl Strom's response after a woman heckler said, "Hey, Earl, If you were my husband, I'd feed you rat poison"

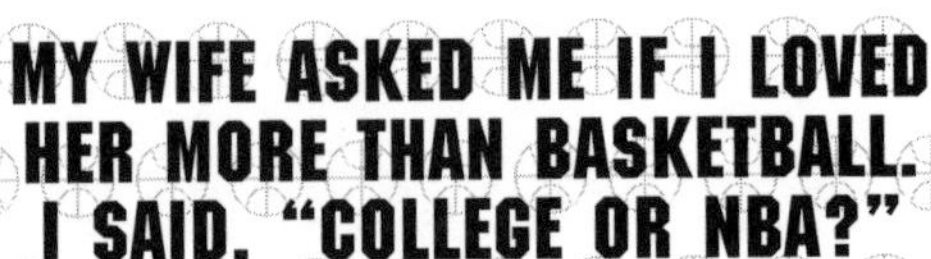

MY WIFE ASKED ME IF I LOVED
HER MORE THAN BASKETBALL.
I SAID, "COLLEGE OR NBA?"

—The Vent column of readers' responses in the *Atlanta Journal-Constitution*

And in an unusual twist, the elephants are the ones complaining about the stench left by their predecessors.

—Elliott Harris of the *Chicago Sun-Times*, on the United Center hosting a circus while the Bulls are on a West Coast trip

If KG is "The Big Ticket," is his half brother "The Ticket Stub"?

—Sheldon Spencer of ESPN.com, on Minnesota Timberwolves forward Kevin Garnett's half brother, Louis McCullough, who plays for Francis Marion University

Word is it works 50 percent of the time.

—Jim Hodges of the *Newport News (VA) Daily Press*, on former Toronto Raptor Vince Carter being featured on the cover of EA Sports' NBA Live video game

A puny lobster-salad sandwich at Boston's FleetCenter costs $10! Ten dollars? For $10 I want my lobster to do a reverse two-and-a-half into a pot of boiling water while whistling the theme from *The Little Mermaid*.

—Rick Reilly of *Sports Illustrated*, on the high cost of attending pro sporting events

Many times at the beach a good-looking lady will say to me, "I want to touch you." I always smile and say, "I don't blame you."

—Former Mr. Universe-turned-California governor Arnold Schwarzenegger

I can't die. It would wreck my image.

—Fitness guru Jack LaLanne, eighty-three, in an interview on HBO's *Real Sports*

Two women were having lunch before their weekly game at the country club. "I just got a great set of golf clubs for my husband," said one. "No kidding?" her friend said incredulously. "That's a great trade!"

—Randy Youngman of the *Orange County Register*

A golfer hooked his tee shot over a hill onto an adjacent fairway. Walking over the hill toward his ball, he saw a man rolling around on the ground, holding his hands over his groin area, groaning in agony. "I'm an attorney," the writhing victim said, "and this is going to cost you $5,000." "I'm very sorry," the remorseful golfer said, "but I did yell, 'Fore!'" Said the attorney: "I'll take it."

—Randy Youngman

Catherine Zeta-Jones, and I would let the other two play through.

—Golfer/TV commentator Gary McCord, when asked who would be in his ultimate foursome

"There's wind rushing from the player's rear." Said shocked fellow announcer Gary McCord: "Excuse me?"

—CBS announcer David Feherty, during the Buick Invitational, on the conditions for Tiger Wood's approach shot to the sixteenth green

About Tiger's impending wedding: How much will he have to pay to find a photographer willing to take the job?

—Jerry Greene of the *Orlando Sentinel*, making reference to Woods having a protective caddie with a temper

The man has ruined more pictures than Sylvester Stallone.

—Rick Reilly of *Sports Illustrated*, after Tiger Woods caddie Steve Williams kicked one photographer's camera and grabbed another at the U.S. Open

There's no word yet as to who will be the best man, but once again Phil Mickelson will probably end up as the bridesmaid.

—Comedian and broadcaster Jim Barach, on Woods' engagement announcement

I've never really had a problem, except when my ex-wives are around.

—Golfer John Daly, on the raucous crowds at the Phoenix Open

Spotted on a fan's T-shirt at Tucson's Corbett Field: "Milwaukee . . . a drinking town . . . with a baseball problem."

—*Arizona Daily Star*

"Do you think anyone played well today, ma'am?" She replied, "Yes, the band."

—Former FA secretary Stanley Rous, escorting Queen Elizabeth to her car following a particularly forgettable soccer cup final at Wembley

We can only guess that Alou's next contract with the Cubs will not be a handshake agreement.

—Chris Dufresne of the *Los Angeles Times*, after Chicago Cubs outfielder Moises Alou revealed that he uses urine on his hands to toughen up his skin

Something tells me Vitali Klitschko isn't going to have one of those cutesy nicknames like Chris Webber (C-Web), Tracy McGrady (T-Mac), or Alex Rodriguez (A-Rod).

—Cam Hutchinson of the *Saskatoon StarPhoenix*

If it would have been the backstroke, I obviously would have stopped.

—Olympic hopeful Matt Zelen, who dived into the pool for the 100-yard butterfly at a big meet in Minnesota, and then realized he had forgotten to tie his racing suit. With his suit sliding off, Zelen kicked it off and finished the race unencumbered. He was disqualified for violating uniform rules.